RAISING STREET-SMART CHRISTIAN KIDS

A PRACTICAL PARENTING PLAYBOOK TO NAVIGATE PEER PRESSURE, STRENGTHEN DISCERNMENT, BUILD STRONG FAITH, AND CHOOSE WISELY IN TODAY'S CULTURE

RADIANT FAITH

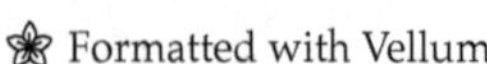 Formatted with Vellum

INTRODUCTION

The Sunday School vs. Monday Morning Gap

Your ten-year-old aced the Bible quiz last week. She can recite the fruits of the Spirit, name all twelve disciples, and tell you exactly why David beat Goliath. Then Monday morning hits. A classmate shows her a TikTok mocking kids who pray before meals. Another friend whispers that believing in God is "weird." By lunch, your daughter sits quietly at the table, unsure whether to bow her head or just eat.

That's the gap most Christian parents feel but struggle to name. Your child knows the right answers on paper, yet those answers can vanish the moment real social pressure shows up. Memorized verses and rehearsed responses work fine in the safety of a church classroom. They fall apart on the school bus, at the sleepover, and in the group chat where everyone's watching.

The reason is simple. Memorization teaches information. It does not build conviction. A child can memorize "be strong and courageous" and still lack the internal grit to actually be strong and courageous when a friend says, "Only babies go to church." That kind of wiring takes more than Sunday morning repetition.

At the same time, there's stiff competition for your child's attention and loyalty. You get a few hours of influence each evening, squeezed between homework and bedtime. TikTok gets unlimited access to a dopamine-driven algorithm that learns exactly what makes your child laugh, agree, and absorb ideas. YouTube creators, school culture, and peer-group dynamics all have a seat at the table, and they serve content 24/7.

If you're parenting a child between eight and twelve, you're in a decisive season. These are the years when your child starts forming opinions that aren't borrowed from yours. They're watching how the world works, deciding who they want to be, and quietly choosing whose voice carries the most weight. That voice will be shaped by the foundation you build, or by whatever rushes in to fill the vacuum.

This isn't here to scare you. It's here to sharpen your focus. The gap between what your child knows and what your child does under pressure is one of the most important areas you can address right now, and closing it takes more than good intentions.

The Street-Smart Christian Framework

So what does it actually look like to raise a child who holds onto faith when it costs something? It usually comes down to two things most parents treat as opposites: high grace and high standards.

With high grace, your home becomes a place where your child can tell the truth without bracing for an explosion. They can tell you about the kid at school who offered them something they shouldn't have, and your first move is to listen instead of launching into a lecture. Connection stays intact even when the conversation gets uncomfortable.

High standards are different. You don't lower the bar because culture calls it old-fashioned. You hold firm expectations around behavior, respect, integrity, and responsibility. Your child knows what the family stands for, and those values aren't up for renegotiation just because something is trending.

Most families lean hard to one side. Grace-heavy homes often produce kids who feel loved but lack structure. Standards-heavy homes can produce kids who behave out of fear but disconnect emotionally. The street-smart Christian framework holds both at once, because that tension is where character gets built.

Think of it like coaching a young athlete. A good coach pushes hard during practice because they see potential. After a tough loss, that same coach puts an arm around the player and says, "We'll get it next time." The push and the presence work together. Without the presence, you can crush a kid. Without the push, you can coddle them.

The second piece of this framework is faith ownership versus routine belief. There's a real difference between a child who goes to church because the family goes and a child who prays on their own because they've seen God come through in a personal way. I've noticed kids take prayer more seriously when they've had even one specific, answered prayer they can name. Routine belief looks like compliance. Faith ownership looks like a twelve-year-old choosing to forgive a friend because they understand what forgiveness costs, even when it stings.

You can't force ownership. What you can do is create the conditions where it has room to grow. That means giving your child space to ask hard questions, wrestle with doubt, and reach conclusions that are genuinely theirs. Proverbs 22:6 says to train up a child in the way they should go. Training involves practice, correction, and repetition in real conditions. It's active, hands-on work.

The third element is independent thinking within biblical boundaries. You want a child who can evaluate what they hear, spot manipulation, and make wise choices without you hovering. But you also want their thinking anchored to something solid. The goal is a kid who can walk into any room, hear any argument, and still think clearly because their internal compass is set to truth.

This framework gives you the structure to build all three: connection, conviction, and discernment. The chapters ahead rest on that foundation.

How to Use This Tactical Playbook

You're busy. You don't have time to read theory for three hundred pages and then guess how to apply it. Each chapter is built to give you something you can use the same day you read it.

Here's how it's set up. Each chapter targets a specific area of your child's development: discipline, faith formation, peer pressure, decision-making, digital media, tough conversations, community building, and preparing for independence. You'll see a familiar rhythm. It starts with a real situation you'll recognize from your own household. Next comes what's really happening under the surface. Then you'll get a biblical principle explained in plain terms, followed by a clear strategy you can put into action.

One of the most useful tools is the "What to Say" scripts scattered throughout these pages. Parenting pressure usually hits hardest in that split second when your child says something that catches you off guard, and you're trying to find the right words without making things worse. These scripts give you exact phrases you can use or tweak. They're built for real conversations, the kind that happen at the kitchen counter, in the car, or right before bed when your child suddenly opens up about something heavy.

You'll also see common mistakes highlighted in each chapter. These are patterns well-meaning parents fall into, often without realizing it. Knowing what to avoid matters just as much as knowing what to do. A small shift in how you respond to pushback, or how you frame a correction, can change the whole dynamic.

At the end of each chapter, you'll find quick action steps. These are one to three specific things you can do right away. They don't require a weekend retreat or a formal family meeting. They're meant to fit into the rhythm of your actual life, because that's where parenting is won or lost.

Now, a word about the age focus. The strategies here are built specifically for kids between eight and twelve. This is the tween and early preteen window, a season when children are ready to reason, question, and form independent thoughts, but they're still emotionally tethered to their parents in ways teenagers often aren't. It's a window of maximum influence and maximum opportunity. The patterns you establish here will shape how your child handles the far more intense pressures of high school and beyond.

If your child is slightly younger or older, you'll still be able to use the principles. The scripts and strategies may need a few small adjustments for a seven-year-old or a fourteen-year-old, but the core approach holds.

One last note before you move on. This playbook works best when you treat it like a system, not a pile of disconnected tips. Each chapter builds on the one before it. The foundation chapter clarifies your family values and emotional regulation. Discipline comes next because it depends on that groundwork. Faith development follows because conviction needs both structure and connection in place. Peer pressure strategies assume your child has started practicing independent thinking. The order is on purpose.

You can skip ahead to the chapter that feels most urgent. If you're in a screen-time battle right now, you may want to go straight to the digital chapter. That's fine. Just know that circling back to the earlier chapters will make the later strategies work better, because the framework supports the whole thing.

You're here because you want more than a well-behaved child. You want a grounded one. A child who can think clearly, stand firm, and carry their faith into rooms where it won't be popular.

Let's start with the foundation.

1

THE FOUNDATION: HIGH STANDARDS WITH HIGH GRACE

Your twelve-year-old daughter comes home from a friend's house and announces she wants to start watching a show that you know is loaded with sexual humor and casual drug references. "Everyone watches it, Mom. It's fine." You feel your jaw tighten. Your husband glances at you from across the kitchen. And in that split second, two competing instincts fire at once: shut it down hard, or avoid the conflict and figure it out later.

This moment, small as it seems, reveals something important. Your response will be shaped by two things: how clear you are on what actually matters in your family, and how well you manage your own emotions in the heat of the moment. Get those two things right, and you'll handle this conversation with confidence. Get them wrong, and you'll either overreact and push your daughter away or underreact and lose ground you can't easily recover.

That's what this chapter is about. Before you can build discipline systems, before you can teach your kids to handle peer pressure or think independently, you need a foundation. And that foundation has two layers: knowing your family's core values with absolute clarity, and developing the emotional steadiness to enforce those values without damaging the relationship.

Core Values vs Flexible Preferences

Most families operate with a vague sense of what they stand for. They know they're "Christian." They know they want their kids to "do the right thing." But when a specific situation hits, that vagueness becomes a problem. You're standing in the kitchen at 8 p.m., making a judgment call about a sleepover, a movie, or a group chat, and you realize you don't have a clear framework to lean on. You end up making decisions based on mood, tiredness, or whatever feels easiest in the moment. One week, you let something slide; the next week, you crack down on the same thing. Your kids notice the inconsistency, and it erodes their trust in your leadership.

The fix is straightforward: separate your non-negotiable biblical convictions from your flexible cultural preferences, and be honest about which is which.

Non-negotiable convictions are rooted in Scripture, and they don't bend with trends. Honesty. Treating others with dignity. Sexual integrity. Respect for authority. Stewardship of what God has given you. These are the load-bearing walls of your family's moral structure. You can explain why they matter. You can point to biblical principles that ground them. And you hold them firmly regardless of what the surrounding culture says. When your son asks why he can't bend the truth to avoid getting a friend in trouble, you have a clear, grounded answer ready. The standard exists before the situation does, which means you're leading proactively instead of scrambling reactively.

Flexible preferences are the things you value, maybe even value deeply, but that come from your own upbringing, personality, or cultural context rather than from clear biblical command. The style of music your kids listen to. Whether they're allowed to trick-or-treat. How they wear their hair. What extracurricular activities they pursue. These things might matter to you, and there's nothing wrong with having opinions about them. But treating preferences with the same weight as convictions creates confusion. Your kids can't tell the difference between "God says this matters" and "Dad just doesn't like rap music." When everything carries the same urgency, nothing carries real weight. Your authority gets diluted because your kids start tuning out every directive equally.

Here's a practical way to sort this out. Sit down with your spouse and write two lists. On the first, put every value you'd be willing to go to the mat for, the things that stay constant no matter what school your kids attend, what neighborhood you live in, or what year it is. On the second list, put the things you care about but could hold loosely if needed. Be ruthless in your honesty. Some things you've been treating as convictions are actually preferences wearing a spiritual costume. That rule about no screens at the dinner table? Probably a wise preference. The expectation that your children speak honestly, even when it costs them something? That's a conviction rooted in the character of God. The distinction matters because your children will eventually push back on both, and you need to know which hills are worth standing on.

Once you've clarified those lists, you're ready to build a family mission statement. Keep it short. One or two sentences that capture who your family is and what you stand for. Something like: "In this family, we tell the truth, we protect each other, and we honor God with how we treat people." Post it somewhere visible. Refer to it when decisions come up. It becomes your family's operating system, the shared language you and your kids use when life gets complicated. When your teenager argues for more freedom, you can point back to the mission statement and say, "Does this decision line up with who we've said we are?" That question reframes the conversation from "me versus you" into "us versus the situation."

Proverbs 22:6 tells you to train up a child in the way they should go. Training requires a clear destination. Your values define that destination. Your preferences are just the route options along the way.

Parental Emotional Regulation First

You can have the clearest values in the world, but if you lose your composure every time your child tests a boundary, those values get drowned out by the noise of your reaction. Kids remember how you made them feel during a correction long after they forget the words you said. And when your emotional state is running the show, you're more likely to say something you'll regret, escalate a small issue into a family crisis, or swing between being too harsh and too lenient.

This is one of the hardest truths in parenting: your emotional regulation matters more than your child's behavior in any given moment. You set the thermostat for the whole house. If you run hot, the entire environment overheats. Your kids will mirror whatever emotional climate you create, whether that's calm confidence or anxious volatility.

Think about what happens when your ten-year-old son lies to your face about whether he finished his homework. Your blood pressure spikes. A voice in your head says, "If he's lying about this now, what will he lie about at sixteen?" Fear kicks in. And fear, left unchecked, comes out as anger. You raise your voice. You pile on consequences. Your son shuts down, and now you've lost the chance to actually address the lying because he's focused on surviving your reaction instead of reflecting on his choice.

The pause-and-pray discipline prep is a simple tool that changes this pattern. When you feel that surge of emotion, you pause. Physically, if you can, step out of the room for thirty seconds. Take a breath. And pray something short and honest: "God, help me respond to this with wisdom, not frustration." You're not asking for a theological download. You're resetting your nervous system and inviting God into the moment before you act. Think of it as calling a timeout before you run the next play. Coaches do this instinctively when emotions are high and the stakes matter. You can do the same thing at your kitchen table.

This pause does three things. First, it breaks the automatic cycle where emotion drives your response. Second, it models self-control for your child, even if they don't realize it in the moment. Third, it protects the relationship. Your correction will land better when it comes from a calm, steady place rather than a reactive one.

Staying calm when your kids push buttons requires you to know your triggers. Maybe it's disrespect. Maybe it's when they ignore you after you've asked three times. Maybe it's the eye roll that makes you feel dismissed. Whatever it is, name it. Write it down if you need to. Talk about it with your spouse so they can help you recognize it in real time. When you know your triggers, they lose some of their power. You can catch yourself thinking, "There it is, the disrespect trigger," and choose a measured response instead of an automatic one.

James 1:19 puts it plainly: be quick to listen, slow to speak, and slow to become angry. That verse is parenting gold, and it starts with you, the adult in the room. Your kids don't need a perfect parent. They need a regulated one. A parent who can hold the line on values without losing control of their own emotions is a parent who earns deep, lasting respect.

One practical adjustment that helps: separate the moment of discovery from the moment of correction. When you find out your daughter lied or your son broke a rule, you don't have to address it right then. You can say, "We're going to talk about this, but I need a few minutes first." That buys you time to calm down, think clearly, and decide on a proportional response. It also sends your child a powerful message: this family handles things thoughtfully, not impulsively.

Authority Plus Connection Balance

Here's where many well-meaning Christian parents get stuck. They know they need to be the authority in their home. Scripture is clear on that. But they also sense that ruling with an iron fist is producing resentment instead of respect. So they swing the other direction, soften everything, and become more friend than parent. Neither extreme works. What your kids need is a parent who is both strong and warm at the same time.

Think of it like a coach who demands excellence from the team but genuinely cares about every player. That coach earns loyalty because the players know two things simultaneously: the standards are real, and they are valued as people. The players run harder for that coach because they trust the relationship behind the expectation. You're building the same dynamic in your home.

Leading with strength means you don't apologize for having standards. You set clear expectations, you enforce consequences consistently, and you don't negotiate on your core values. When your thirteen-year-old pushes back on a boundary, you hold it. You don't need to yell. You don't need to over-explain. A calm, firm "I understand you disagree, and the answer is still no" carries more authority than a ten-minute lecture ever will.

Leading with warmth means your kids know, deep in their bones, that your love for them is constant and unconditional. It means you're approachable. It means they can come to you with hard things without expecting an explosion. Warmth looks like sitting on the edge of your son's bed at night and asking, "How are you really doing?" It looks like laughing together, being curious about their world, and responding to their honesty with gratitude instead of panic.

Building respect without crushing your child's spirit requires you to correct the behavior while affirming the person. There's a massive difference between "You lied, and that's unacceptable in this family. We're going to deal with this," and "I can't believe you'd do that. What's wrong with you?" The first statement addresses the action and holds the standard. The second attacks the child's identity. Over time, identity attacks don't produce better behavior. They produce kids who hide everything from you because vulnerability feels too risky.

Creating a safe environment for honest conversations is one of the most strategic things you can do as a parent. When your daughter tells you she saw something inappropriate online, your reaction in that moment determines whether she'll come to you next time. If you freak out, ground her, and take her phone away on the spot, she learns that honesty leads to punishment. If you stay calm, thank her for telling you, and then work through the situation together, she learns that honesty leads to help. You still address the issue. You still might adjust her screen access. But you do it in a way that rewards transparency rather than penalizing it.

A script that works well in these moments: "Thank you for telling me that. I know it wasn't easy. Let's figure out what to do about it together." Those three sentences communicate warmth, respect, and partnership. They keep the door open for future conversations. And they position you as a trusted guide rather than a warden. Over months and years, these moments compound. Each time your child brings you something hard and walks away feeling heard, you're reinforcing a pattern that will serve your family through the turbulent seasons ahead.

Ephesians 6:4 instructs parents not to provoke their children to anger, but to bring them up in the training and instruction of the Lord. That verse holds both halves of the equation. Training and instruction require authority. Avoiding provocation requires connection and emotional awareness. When you hold both in balance, you create a home where your kids feel safe enough to be honest and challenged enough to grow.

One common mistake here is inconsistency between parents. If one parent plays the heavy and the other plays the softie, kids learn to work the system. They go to whichever parent is more likely to give the answer they want. Get on the same page with your spouse. Agree on the non-negotiables. Present a united front, even if you disagree on the details, and hash out those disagreements privately.

Playbook Implementation: Family Values Blueprint

Put this into practice this week with three concrete steps.

Step One: The Values Identification Exercise. Set aside thirty minutes with your spouse. Each of you independently writes down ten values you consider essential for your family. Then compare lists. Circle the ones that overlap. Discuss the ones that don't. Narrow it down to five to seven core values you both agree are non-negotiable. Write them down clearly and keep the list somewhere accessible.

Step Two: The Family Contract. Once you've identified your core values, create a simple family agreement. Include the values, the expectations tied to each one, and the general consequences for violating them. Keep the language plain. Read it together as a family. Let your kids ask questions. Have everyone sign it. This isn't a legal document; it's a shared commitment that makes the invisible rules of your home visible and fair.

Step Three: The Quarterly Review. Every three months, revisit the contract as a family. Ask: Are these values still clear? Are the expectations realistic for the ages of our kids? Do we need to adjust consequences? Your eight-year-old and your fourteen-year-old don't need the same rules, and what works in September might need tweaking by January. This review keeps the system alive and shows your kids that your leadership is thoughtful, not rigid. It also gives your children a voice in the process, which builds their ownership of the family's standards rather than breeding resentment toward rules they had no part in shaping.

These three actions give you a working blueprint. Values without a system stay abstract. A system without values becomes mechanical. When you combine clear convictions, emotional steadiness, and an authority-plus-connection approach, you build a foundation strong enough to support every strategy that follows. The conversations get easier. The boundaries hold with less friction. And your kids begin to internalize the values you've been modeling, which is the ultimate goal of every principle in this playbook.

2

THE DISCIPLINE FRAMEWORK: CONSEQUENCES THAT BUILD CHARACTER

Your ten-year-old didn't do his homework. You found out at 8:47 p.m. because the teacher sent an email. You walked into his room, and before you could finish your first sentence, he fired back: "It's not even due tomorrow." You corrected him. He rolled his eyes. You raised your voice. He matched it. Within ninety seconds, the conversation had nothing to do with homework anymore. It turned into a contest of wills, complete with door-slamming and that awful silence that fills the house afterward.

Sound familiar? You're not alone, and you're not failing. But the cycle has to stop. The good news is there's a way through it, and it's learnable.

The Power Struggle Elimination System

Power struggles between parents and tweens tend to follow the same track. Your child says or does something that crosses a line. You correct it. They push back. You push harder. They escalate. You escalate. Before long, both of you are angry, and the original issue is buried under layers of frustration. The real problem was never the homework or the chores or the attitude. The problem is that the interaction became a competition, and nobody wins a competition between a parent and their child.

Here's what's usually happening under the surface. Between the ages of eight and twelve, your child is building a sturdier sense of self. They test boundaries because their brain is leaning hard toward independence. That's healthy. The trouble starts when every correction turns into a debate. Then your child learns that pushing back long enough, or loud enough, gets results. Either you give in, or the conversation derails so completely that the expectation disappears. Both outcomes teach the same lesson: resistance works.

Proverbs 15:1 puts it plainly: "A gentle answer turns away wrath, but a harsh word stirs up anger." That's not abstract wisdom. It's for your Tuesday night standoff. When you match your child's energy, you add fuel. When you stay calm and hold the line, the fire starts to die out.

The first tool you need is what parenting strategists call the broken record technique. It's simple. You state the expectation once, clearly. When your child argues, you repeat the expectation using nearly the same words, without adding new information, without raising your voice, and without engaging in the argument. You sound like a broken record on purpose.

Here's what this looks like in real life. Your daughter was supposed to clean her room before screen time. She didn't. You say: "Your room needs to be cleaned before you use the tablet." She responds with, "I'll do it after the show." You say: "Your room needs to be cleaned before you use the tablet." She says, "That's so unfair, Mom. Everyone else gets to watch first." You say: "I hear you. Your room needs to be cleaned before you use the tablet." No debate. No explanation of why the rule exists. No defending yourself. The same sentence, delivered calmly, every single time.

Most parents make the mistake of adding new reasoning to each response. "Because I told you to." "Because you promised." "Because that's the rule in this house." Each new sentence gives your child something fresh to argue against. The broken record technique removes that material. There's nothing to grab onto, so the argument runs out of traction.

For this to work, your tone has to stay steady. You're a thermostat, not a thermometer. A thermometer reacts to the temperature in the room. A thermostat sets it. Your calm, consistent repetition sets the emotional temperature of the interaction.

Here are three scripts you can use tonight for immediate compliance without debate:

Script 1 (Chore resistance): "The dishes need to be done before free time. I'll be in the kitchen when you're ready." Then walk away. Don't stand there waiting for agreement.

Script 2 (Homework avoidance): "Homework comes first. You can choose to start now or in five minutes, but it gets done before anything else." Give the timeline, then disengage.

Script 3 (Bedtime pushback): "It's time for bed. You can read for ten minutes or go straight to sleep. That's your choice." Offer a small choice within the boundary, then hold it.

Notice the pattern in each script: state the expectation, offer a limited choice when possible, then remove yourself from the argument. You're not giving your child the stage they need to perform. You're closing the curtain calmly and walking backstage.

One common mistake is confusing disengagement with disconnection. Walking away from an argument is strategic. Ignoring your child's feelings is harmful. After the task is done and the tension has passed, circle back. A simple, "I know that felt frustrating. I'm glad you got it done," reinforces the boundary without turning the relationship into collateral damage.

Natural vs. Logical Consequences for Tweens

Consequences are the engine of discipline, but the wrong consequence at the wrong time teaches nothing. When you understand the difference between natural and logical consequences, choosing the right response gets much simpler.

A natural consequence is what happens on its own when you step out of the way. Your son forgets his lunch at home. He goes hungry until snack time. Your daughter doesn't study for her test. She gets a poor grade. You didn't create the consequence. Reality did. Your job in those moments is to resist the urge to rescue. That's harder than it sounds, especially when your child calls from school sounding desperate. But every rescue teaches your child that someone else will clean up the mess. Every time you let the natural consequence play out, your child learns that actions have weight.

A logical consequence is one you create because the natural consequence is either too dangerous, too delayed, or basically nonexistent. If your child lies about finishing their chores, the natural consequence of a messy room doesn't carry enough weight to address the dishonesty. So you create a logical consequence: extra chores the next day, or a temporary loss of a privilege tied to the behavior. The key word is "tied." Logical consequences have to connect directly to what happened, or they feel random and punitive to your child.

Here's a quick test: Can your child draw a straight line between what they did and what happened next? If your child left their bike in the driveway and loses bike privileges for two days, that line is clear. If your child left their bike in the driveway and loses dessert, that line doesn't exist. The consequence feels like punishment for its own sake, and punishment without connection breeds resentment.

Now let's talk about the topic a lot of parents of tweens dread: technology removal. Taking away a phone, tablet, or gaming console can feel like declaring war. Your child may react as though you removed a limb. The tears, the anger, the accusations of unfairness can make you wonder if it was worth it. It can be, but the way you do it matters.

First, don't take away technology in the heat of an argument. When you grab the phone mid-conflict, it lands as retaliation. Your child focuses on your anger, not their behavior. Instead, cool down first.

Then sit with your child and explain the connection between the behavior and the consequence.

Try this script: "You used your phone past the agreed time three nights in a row. Because of that, the phone stays with me from 7 p.m. to morning for the rest of the week. On Monday, we'll reset." Notice the specificity. You named the behavior. You named the consequence. You gave a clear end date. Open-ended consequences feel like prison sentences to a tween and often lead to more resentment and defiance than clear, time-bound ones. I've seen the temperature in a home drop fast once a kid knows exactly when they'll get the privilege back.

Second, build responsibility through strategic choices. Instead of only removing privileges, create a way for your child to earn them back through demonstrated responsibility. If your son lost screen time because he didn't finish his homework, let him earn an extra thirty minutes on Saturday by completing all assignments on time for three consecutive days. That shifts discipline from something done to your child into something your child has real agency within.

Galatians 6:7 says, "A man reaps what he sows." That principle clicks for your child when consequences follow behavior with consistency and clarity. You're teaching them a spiritual truth through everyday experience: choices have outcomes, and they're the ones making the choices.

A mistake many parents make with consequences is inconsistency. You enforce the rule on Monday but let it slide on Wednesday because you're tired. Your child notices. They learn that persistence pays off, and that if they push at the right moment, the rule bends. Consistency doesn't mean perfection. It means that when you set a consequence, you follow through most of the time. If you realize a consequence was too harsh or didn't make sense, adjust it out loud. Say, "I thought about it, and here's what I'm changing and why." That models integrity. Quietly dropping consequences models something else.

Addressing Defiance Without Crushing Spirit

There's a moment every parent recognizes. Your child looks you square in the eye and says, "No." Or they mutter under their breath. Or they do exactly what you asked them not to do, while watching for your reaction. Defiance feels personal. It triggers something deep in most parents because it can feel like a direct challenge to your authority, your values, and sometimes your worth.

Take a breath. Defiance in a tween is often a clumsy attempt to assert independence, not a calculated attack on your authority. That doesn't make it acceptable. It does change how you respond.

The goal of correction in these moments is twofold: address the behavior clearly and keep the relationship intact. You can do both. Ephesians 6:4 instructs parents not to provoke their children to anger but to bring them up in training and instruction. Training means teaching. Teaching requires a student who is willing to listen. If your correction humiliates your child or crushes their spirit, you lose the student.

Here's a script for respectful correction when defiance shows up: "I can see you're upset, and we'll talk about that. Right now, what I need you to do is [specific action]. We can discuss how you feel about it after." This does two things. It names the emotion without approving the behavior, and it keeps the expectation front and center.

What you want to avoid is the lecture spiral. You know the one. It starts with the behavior and somehow ends with a fifteen-minute review of every mistake your child has made that month. Lectures shut tweens down quickly, often within the first minute, as their attention fades and resistance builds. Keep corrections to two or three sentences. Say what happened, say what you expect, and say what the consequence will be if it continues. Then stop.

Teaching self-correction and ownership is the long game here, and it's one of the most valuable skills your child can develop. After an incident of defiance, once things have cooled down (give it at least thirty minutes, sometimes longer), come back and ask two questions: "What happened?" and "What would you do differently next time?" These questions shift the processing from external (you telling them what went wrong) to internal (them identifying it themselves). The first few times you try this, expect short answers. "I don't know" is a classic. Resist the urge to fill the silence. Wait. Let them think. Over time, they'll get better at this, and that skill transfers into every area of their life.

Rebuilding the relationship after discipline is the step most parents skip, and it may be the most important one. Once the consequence is delivered and the conversation is done, find a way to reconnect. It doesn't have to be elaborate. Sit next to them for five minutes. Ask about something unrelated to the conflict. Make their favorite snack. The message is simple: the boundary is real, and so is your love.

A common mistake is using affection as leverage. Withdrawing warmth after discipline, giving the cold shoulder, or making your child feel they need to earn their way back into the relationship teaches them that closeness is conditional. That's not what you want to train into them. God disciplines those He loves, and His love doesn't waver. Your discipline should follow that pattern.

One more mistake to watch for: apologizing for holding the boundary. If the consequence was fair and the delivery was respectful, you have nothing to apologize for. Saying, "I'm sorry I had to do that," undercuts what you just set in place. If you genuinely overcorrected or lost your temper, then yes, apologize for that specific behavior. "I shouldn't have raised my voice. I'm sorry for that. The consequence still stands." That's honest. It's steady. And it shows your child what accountability looks like.

Playbook Implementation: Power-Struggle Prevention Drill

Everything above is easy to agree with and hard to use when you're tired, stressed, and trying to get everyone to bed. You need a system on paper that you can reference, adjust, and share with anyone who helps raise your kids. Here's how to build it.

Consequence Planning Worksheet

Sit down this week and list the five most common behavior issues in your home. For each one, write out the expected behavior, the natural consequence (if one exists), and a logical consequence you'll use if needed. Keep it simple. One page, five rows. Here's an example of how one row looks:

Behavior issue: Refusing to do homework. Expected behavior: Homework completed before screen time. Natural consequence: Lower grades over time. Logical consequence: No screens until homework is finished; if lying about completion occurs, an additional day without screens.

Fill out all five rows. Post this somewhere you can see it. Then, when a situation hits, you're not inventing consequences in the moment. You've already decided.

Family Discipline Policy Template

This is a one-page document you create with your spouse or co-parent, and eventually share with your kids in age-appropriate language. It covers three things:

Our family values: List three to five core values that drive your household. Keep them concrete. "We tell the truth." "We treat each other with respect." "We finish what we start."

Our expectations: For each value, name one or two specific behaviors that reflect it. "Telling the truth means no lying about homework, chores, or where you've been."

Our consequences: For each expectation, state what happens when it's met and what happens when it's broken. "When you complete homework on time, you get full screen privileges. When you don't, screens are paused until it's done."

Share this with your kids during a calm, neutral time. A Saturday morning usually works better than a Monday night after a blowup. Walk them through it. Let them ask questions. When they know the system ahead of time, consequences feel less like ambushes and more like the next step in a process they already understand.

Daily Implementation Checklist

Use this three-item checklist each evening to keep the system running:

1. Did I follow through on every consequence I set today? If not, make a note and correct it tomorrow.
2. Did I stay calm during at least one moment that could have escalated? Acknowledge that win, even if the day was rough overall.
3. Did I reconnect with my child after any corrections that happened today? If not, do it before bedtime. A simple "I love you" and a normal conversation about tomorrow can do more than another speech.

Run this checklist for twenty-one consecutive days to build momentum. Full habits often take longer (researcher Phillippa Lally's 2009 study at University College London found an average of 66 days), but three weeks is usually enough to make this feel less like a big new project and more like something you actually do.

Your action steps for this week: First, write out your five-row consequence planning worksheet tonight. Second, draft your family discipline policy and review it with your co-parent before sharing it with your kids. Third, start the daily checklist tomorrow evening and keep it going for twenty-one days straight.

3

DEVELOPING REAL FAITH: FROM SUNDAY SCHOOL TO STREET SMART

Your twelve-year-old sits in the back seat after Wednesday night youth group, scrolling through his phone. You ask how it went. "Fine," he says. You push a little. "What did you guys talk about?" He shrugs. "I don't know. Faith stuff." That's the whole conversation. He's been going to church since he was in diapers. He can recite John 3:16 from memory, knows the story of David and Goliath inside and out, and sings along during worship without complaint. On paper, everything looks solid. But that shrug stays with you the rest of the evening. Because deep down, you're wondering: does he actually believe any of this for himself, or is he just going through the motions because we've always done it this way?

That question matters more than most parents think. A child who has memorized all the right answers but has never personally wrestled with why those answers are true is standing on borrowed faith. And borrowed faith has an expiration date. It often runs out somewhere between freshman year of high school and the second semester of college, right when the pressure to fit in is highest, and your direct influence is lowest. The goal is simple: help your child move from "my parents believe this" to "I believe this, and here's why." That shift changes how they handle temptation, peer pressure, and the hard questions life will throw at them.

The Faith Ownership Test

There's a meaningful difference between a child who believes in God because you told them to and a child who believes in God because they've thought it through and made it personal. Both kids can look the same on Sunday morning. They'll both bow their heads during prayer, sing the songs, and answer the small group questions. The difference shows up on Tuesday afternoon when a friend says, "Church is for weak people," or on Friday night when everyone else is making choices that go against what they've been taught.

So how do you know which kind of faith your child is developing? Start by watching for a few indicators. A child who owns their faith will occasionally bring up God or spiritual topics without being prompted. They'll ask questions that go beyond the surface, like "Why does God let bad things happen?" or "How do we know the Bible is actually true?" Those questions might catch you off guard, but they're often a sign of healthy engagement. A child running on inherited belief alone rarely asks hard questions because they've never felt the need to. They accept the package as delivered.

Another sign is how your child responds when faith costs them something. If your son turns down an invitation because he knows the situation conflicts with his values, and he does it without needing you to make the call, that's ownership. If your daughter stands by a classmate being mocked and later tells you she felt it was the right thing to do because of something she read in Proverbs, that's conviction, not just compliance.

On the other hand, watch for warning signs. A child who only talks about God when you initiate the conversation, who treats church attendance like a chore on par with taking out the trash, or who can give you textbook answers but seems disconnected from the meaning behind them is probably operating on autopilot. That's not a crisis. It's a growth opportunity. You're noticing it now, which means you can respond while the door is still open.

Here are a few questions you can use to gauge where your child stands. You don't need to sit them down for a formal interview. Work these into normal conversations over dinner, during car rides, or before bed.

"If your friends asked you why you believe in God, what would you say?"

"Is there anything about our faith that confuses you or that you're not sure about?"

"When was the last time you prayed about something on your own, without anyone reminding you?"

"Do you think God actually cares about the stuff going on in your life right now? Why or why not?"

Listen carefully to their answers, and resist the urge to correct them on the spot if something sounds off. You're trying to understand where they are, because you can't guide someone to a destination if you don't know their starting point. Deuteronomy 6:6-7 tells parents to impress God's commands on their children's hearts, talking about them at home, on the road, at bedtime, and in the morning. The emphasis isn't on formal instruction alone. It's on consistent, everyday conversations woven into real life. That's where faith starts moving from your heart to theirs.

Moving your child beyond inherited belief means giving them room to question, wrestle, and arrive at their own conclusions within the boundaries you've set. You're not removing the guardrails. You're teaching them to drive inside those guardrails because they want to, not because they have to.

Biblical Critical Thinking for Real Life

Teaching your child to think theologically can sound academic. In real life, it's one of the most practical skills you can help them build.

Thinking theologically means your child can look at a situation and ask, "What would God say about this?" or "What does Scripture tell me about how to handle this?" It becomes a filter they run decisions through before they act.

Most kids already have filters. They run choices through what their friends think, what social media labels as cool, and what feels good in the moment. Your job is to help them develop a stronger one, rooted in biblical truth, that kicks in before those other voices get the first say.

Start with real situations, not hypotheticals. When your child comes home and tells you about drama at school, a friend who got caught cheating, a classmate being excluded, or a rumor making the rounds, don't rush to give your take. Ask what they think first. Then you can guide the conversation toward Scripture without turning the kitchen table into a pulpit.

You might say, "That's a tough situation. What do you think the right thing to do would be?" After they answer, connect it: "You know, there's a verse in Galatians that talks about this kind of thing. It says to carry each other's burdens. What do you think that could look like for your friend right now?" You've done something important here. You let them think first, then you showed them the Bible speaks into the exact kind of mess they're dealing with today. Over time, they start making that connection on their own.

Scripture application works best when it's tied to decisions your child is already facing. A ten-year-old dealing with a bossy friend doesn't need a lecture on Philippians 2. He needs you to read that passage with him and talk about what it looks like to put someone else's interests ahead of your own when that someone is being difficult. A thirteen-year-old trying to decide whether to go along with what everyone else is watching online needs you to walk through Romans 12:2 in a way that lands on her Tuesday night, not just her Sunday morning.

Building a biblical worldview happens the same way. You don't sit down and teach it like a subject. You shape it, conversation by conversation, over years. When your family watches the news together, and your child sees something disturbing, help them process it through

Scripture. "Why do you think that happened? What does the Bible say about how people should treat each other? What would it look like if someone actually lived that out at school tomorrow?" Those kinds of questions train your child to interpret the world through a biblical frame instead of absorbing whatever story the culture is selling.

One practical approach is a weekly "real life, real faith" check-in. Pick one thing that happened during the week, something at school, something in the news, or something between siblings, and spend ten minutes connecting it to a biblical principle. Keep it short. Ten minutes is enough, and, honestly, it's the only length I've seen work consistently in most families. You're not preaching. You're coaching your child to think. Over months and years, that habit becomes more natural.

A common mistake is using Scripture only as a correction tool. If the Bible only shows up when your child is in trouble, they'll associate it with punishment instead of guidance. Bring Scripture into the good moments, too. When something goes well, when your child shows kindness or makes a wise choice, tie it back: "You know what you just did? That's exactly what Micah 6:8 talks about. Acting justly and loving mercy. That was the real deal." Now the Bible isn't just a rulebook in your child's mind. It's guidance for how to live.

Spiritual Disciplines That Stick

Prayer and Bible reading are the backbone of any growing faith. But this is where a lot of well-meaning families hit a wall. They make spiritual disciplines feel like homework. When devotions become another checklist item right after "brush your teeth" and "finish your math," kids learn to endure them rather than engage. The discipline turns dutiful instead of personal.

Start with age-appropriate expectations. An eight-year-old doesn't need a thirty-minute quiet time. Five minutes of focused prayer and one short passage of Scripture, read together, is plenty. A twelve-year-old can handle a little more independence, maybe a short devotional they read on their own with a five-minute family discussion afterward.

A fourteen-year-old can begin journaling prayers or reading a chapter of Proverbs each day. The key is matching the practice to the child's developmental stage so it feels doable, not crushing.

For prayer specifically, teach your kids to pray about real things. Young children often get stuck in the "God bless Mommy, God bless Daddy, God bless the dog" loop because that's what they've heard. Push beyond that. Ask your child, "What's one thing that's bugging you right now?" Then say, "Let's talk to God about that." When prayer touches actual concerns, such as nerves about a test, frustration with a friend, or sadness about something that happened at school, it becomes a living conversation instead of a ritual.

Model it too. When you're driving, and something stressful happens, pray out loud, briefly, right there. "Lord, give me patience with this traffic and help me stay calm." Your child hears it and learns something important: prayer isn't reserved for mealtimes and bedtimes. It's for real time, in real life.

Bible reading follows the same principle. Keep it practical, not ceremonial. Instead of grinding through a reading plan that feels disconnected, try linking your family's reading to something your child is facing. If your kid is anxious about starting a new school, read Psalm 56:3 together: "When I am afraid, I put my trust in you." Then talk about what that trust looks like in plain terms. What does it look like to trust God when you're walking into a cafeteria full of strangers? Get specific. Get concrete.

Connecting faith to Monday morning choices is where it all either sticks or fades. The real test of spiritual disciplines is whether they shape what your child does when you're not watching. That connection gets built through consistency and conversation. Every time you help your child tie a spiritual truth to a real decision, you strengthen the bridge between Sunday learning and weekday living.

Here's an example. Your daughter is upset because she wasn't invited to a birthday party, and all her other friends were. She's hurt, angry, and already planning how to get back at the girl who excluded her. This is a spiritual discipline moment, even though it doesn't feel like one. Sit with her. Name the hurt. Then ask, "What do you think God would want you to do with this feeling?" You're not dismissing her pain. You're guiding her toward a response. If she's been practicing prayer as a real conversation with God, she may already have the instinct to bring it to Him. If she's been reading about forgiveness and kindness, she'll have a starting point for what to do next.

The mistakes to avoid here are significant. First, don't force it. A child who's made to pray through gritted teeth isn't developing spiritual maturity. They're building resentment. If your kid pushes back on devotions, shorten them, change the format, or try a different time of day. Flexibility with the method protects the mission. Second, don't make spiritual disciplines a solo assignment for young children. Kids under twelve, especially, benefit from doing these things with you. Your presence communicates that this matters to you personally, which carries more weight than any lecture. Third, don't skip the application piece. Reading a Bible verse without talking about how it lands in your child's actual life is like reading a recipe without ever cooking the meal.

Scripts for Faith Doubts and Hard Questions

Your child will ask hard questions. When they do, your response in that moment shapes whether they see you as a safe place to process doubt or someone they need to hide their questions from. Here are scripts for the three most common faith challenges.

When your child asks, "How do you know God is even real?" stay calm. Don't panic, and don't shut it down. Say something like: "That's a good question, and most people ask it at some point. I believe God is real because of what I've experienced in my own life, and because of what I see in creation and Scripture. But I want you to work through this for yourself. Let's look at it together. What's making you wonder about it right now?" That last question matters. Often, the real issue underneath isn't philosophical. It's personal. Maybe a prayer felt unanswered. Maybe a friend made fun of them for believing. Get to the root.

When the topic of science versus faith comes up, and it will, resist the urge to frame it as a war. Try this: "Science and faith are asking different kinds of questions. Science asks how things work. Faith asks why things exist and what they mean. A lot of brilliant scientists throughout history have been people of deep faith. Let's look at what the Bible says about creation and compare it with what you're learning in class. I think you'll find they fit together more than you'd expect." This positions you as a thoughtful guide, not someone who dismisses your child's education.

When your child struggles with suffering and injustice, saying "It's all part of God's plan" will fall flat, especially if they're personally affected. Instead, try: "I don't have a neat answer for why this happened. What I do know is that God is present in suffering, and He promises to bring good even out of terrible things. That doesn't make the pain less real. It means we're not alone in it. How are you feeling about what happened? Let's talk through it." Honesty about your limits builds more trust than a confident answer that doesn't ring true.

Playbook Implementation: Faith Internalization Exercise

Put this into practice this week with two simple actions.

First, start a weekly faith conversation using one of these prompts at dinner or during a car ride: "What's something you learned about God this week that surprised you?" or "If you could ask God one question and get an answer right now, what would it be?" or "Did anything happen this week where you felt like God was part of it?" Rotate through these and add your own over time. The consistency matters more than the depth of any single conversation.

Second, have your child begin a one-page "What I Believe and Why" worksheet. At the top, they write one thing they believe about God. Underneath, they write their reason in their own words. One belief per week. Over a few months, they'll build a personal statement of faith that sounds like them, not like a memorized script.

4

THE PEER PRESSURE PLAYBOOK: STANDING FIRM AGAINST THE CROWD

Your twelve-year-old comes home from school quieter than usual. Over dinner, she barely touches her food. Later that night, you overhear her on a video call with a friend saying, "Fine, I'll do it, just stop asking." You don't know what "it" is yet, but the tone in her voice tells you enough. She's caving. She knows it. She hates how it feels, but she doesn't know what else to do.

This moment shows up in some form in almost every household. Sometimes it's loud and obvious. More often, it's quiet, slow, and invisible until the consequences surface. It builds in layers so thin that neither you nor your child notices until the weight becomes undeniable. Peer pressure doesn't always show up as a kid on the playground daring your child to steal something. Now it looks like a group chat that won't stop pinging, a friend who says "you're being dramatic" every time your child sets a limit, or an unspoken social code that punishes anyone who won't go along.

The deeper issue is that most kids haven't been taught to recognize pressure while it's happening, and they haven't practiced what to do in the moment. They understand the concept in theory. They've heard "just say no" a hundred times. But when they're standing in a circle of friends at a sleepover, or staring at a screen full of messages pushing them toward something that feels wrong, the theory disappears. The gap between knowing the right answer and actually saying it under social heat is enormous. That gap is where a lot of kids get swallowed up. What they need is a system: the ability to spot manipulation, the confidence to hold a line, and the practiced language to do it without becoming a social outcast.

That's what this chapter gives you.

The Peer Audit: Spotting Manipulation

Before your child can stand firm, they need to see clearly. A lot of kids miss manipulation because it comes wrapped in friendship. The person pressuring them is usually someone they care about, someone they eat lunch with, someone whose opinion carries weight. That's exactly why it works.

You can teach your child to run what we'll call a "peer audit." Think of it as a routine check-up for their friendships. You're helping them get into the habit of noticing how specific relationships actually make them feel, rather than assuming every friend has their best interests in mind.

Start by helping them spot the red flags. A friend who only reaches out when they want something. A group that uses guilt or exclusion to control behavior. Someone who mocks your child's values, even "jokingly," to stir up shame. A person who shares your child's private information to gain social leverage. These patterns don't always look dramatic. They tend to show up as small, repeated moments that quietly reshape your child's sense of normal. Maybe it's the friend who always "jokes" about your daughter's clothes until she starts dressing differently just to avoid the comments. Maybe it's the buddy who calls your son soft every time he doesn't want to look at something online. Each moment seems minor on its own. Stacked together over weeks and months, they change what your child starts to accept.

Here's a concrete way to teach this. Sit down with your child and ask them to think about three or four of their closest friends. For each one, ask simple questions: "Do you feel better or worse about yourself after spending time with them?" "Have they ever asked you to do something you weren't comfortable with?" "Do they respect it when you say no, or do they push harder?" You're training observation, not suspicion. The goal is to help your child build an honest internal gauge for the health of their relationships. If they struggle to answer, that's useful information. It usually means they haven't been paying attention to the emotional dynamics around them, which is exactly why this exercise exists. Keep the tone curious and relaxed. You're exploring together, like reviewing game film after a match.

Pressure tactics in the tween and teen years tend to follow a few predictable patterns. The first is the "everyone's doing it" appeal, which replaces a child's judgment with group consensus. The second is the loyalty test, where a friend frames compliance as proof of friendship: "If you were really my friend, you'd come." The third is social shaming, where a child is mocked or excluded for setting a boundary. The fourth is the slow drip, where small compromises are requested over time until the child wakes up miles from where they started and can't pinpoint when the turn happened. Think of it like a GPS that recalculates by one degree every few days. At first, the route looks almost identical. Six months later, your child is headed somewhere else entirely.

Proverbs 13:20 puts it plainly: "Walk with the wise and become wise, for a companion of fools suffers harm." You don't need to preach this to your child. You need to help them see it playing out in real time, inside their own social circles. When they can name the pattern, they can resist it. When it stays invisible, it runs the show.

Age matters here. A seven- or eight-year-old needs help understanding that a real friend doesn't say, "I won't be your friend anymore if you don't." That's a simple boundary to teach. A twelve-year-old needs more nuance. They need to understand that pressure can be silent and that it can come through what's expected rather than what's said. A fourteen-year-old needs to recognize that sometimes the pressure comes from someone they have romantic feelings for, which makes it even harder to resist.

Set the expectation early: your child always has permission to blame you. "My mom checks my phone" or "My dad will find out" might sound uncool, but it gives your child an exit ramp that saves face. You become the bad guy, so they don't have to be. That's a small sacrifice worth making every time.

Building an Internal Validation System

Here's the harder truth. Even if your child can spot every manipulation tactic in the playbook, they'll still fold if their sense of worth depends on the approval of the people pressuring them. The ability to resist peer pressure isn't primarily a skill problem. It's an identity problem.

Kids who constantly look to friends, social media, or popularity to feel good about themselves will stay vulnerable. Their emotional stability depends on a source they can't control. One day they're accepted, the next day they're out of the group chat. That kind of volatility wears a child down until they'll do almost anything to keep the approval flowing.

Your job is to help your child build what amounts to an internal validation system. Think of it like an internal compass that keeps pointing to a fixed reference point, no matter what happens around them. For a Christian family, that fixed point is their identity in Christ.

That sounds spiritual, because it is. It's also practical. A child who truly believes they have value because God made them with purpose, not because a group of thirteen-year-olds included them at lunch, will respond to pressure differently. They carry a steadiness that other kids can sense. You've met adults like this. They walk into tense situations and stay grounded because their worth was settled long before the room formed an opinion. They still feel the pull. They still want to belong. They're human. But their core sense of self isn't renegotiated in every social interaction.

Building this system takes time and repetition. It won't come from one conversation. It comes from consistent deposits into your child's identity account. Every time you affirm something specific about their character, you're reinforcing a truth that competes with the crowd's message. "I noticed you were patient with your sister today. That takes real self-control." "You chose to be honest even when it was uncomfortable. That's the kind of person you're becoming." These statements anchor your child's identity in observable character traits, not in how well they perform socially. Consistency matters more than eloquence here. A short, genuine observation offered regularly will shape your child far more than an occasional heartfelt speech. Each affirmation is a brick. One brick doesn't do much. Hundreds of them, placed over years, build a wall that peer pressure has a hard time getting through.

One practical idea is to teach your child the difference between "audience of one" living and "audience of everyone" living. When your child makes a choice based on what God sees and what they know is right, they're answering to a consistent, unchanging standard. When they make choices based on what their friend group thinks, they're chasing a target that moves every week. Even kids as young as nine can grasp this when you put it in terms they recognize: "Who are you trying to impress right now? And does their opinion of you change based on what you do for them?"

Romans 12:2 gives language for it: "Do not conform to the pattern of this world, but be transformed by the renewing of your mind." For your child, "the pattern of this world" often looks like the social hierarchy of their school, their team, or their online community. The "renewing of their mind" happens when they regularly return to a different standard of measurement. In real life, that can look like weekly conversations where you help your child evaluate recent decisions: "What choices did you make this week because you believed they were right? What choices did you make because someone else expected them?" That distinction, repeated over months, trains your child to check their motivations while things are happening, not just afterward.

You can reinforce this in everyday moments. When your child is upset because a friend left them out, resist the urge to immediately fix the social problem. Pause and ask, "Does this change who you are?" When your child is thrilled because they got invited to the popular group, celebrate with them, and then ask, "What do you think they value about you? Is it the kind of thing that actually matters?"

A common mistake parents make is trying to replace peer validation with parental validation. If your child's sense of worth simply shifts from "my friends think I'm cool" to "my parents think I'm great," you haven't solved the problem. You've only moved the dependency. The goal is self-worth rooted deeper than any human opinion, including yours. You're pointing them toward God's assessment of who they are, which doesn't shift with social trends or mood swings.

Teach your child to separate feelings from facts. They will feel rejected sometimes. They will feel like they don't belong. Those feelings are real, but they aren't the final word on their value. The fact is that they were made on purpose, with specific gifts, for a reason that doesn't depend on anyone else's vote. Help them build a short list of truths they can return to when the feelings hit hard, three or four sentences they know are true regardless of the social weather: "God made me on purpose." "My value doesn't change based on who includes me." "I can handle feeling left out without falling apart." These become mental anchors they can grab when the emotional current tries to pull them off course.

Role-Playing Common Scenarios

Knowledge and identity matter, but your child also needs rehearsed responses. When pressure hits in real time, the brain defaults to whatever has been practiced. If your child has never said the words out loud, they often won't come out when the moment arrives. This is why athletes practice plays before the game, and it's why your family needs to practice too. Navy SEALs train in conditions that simulate combat stress because, under pressure, the brain reaches for what it has rehearsed, and not much else. Your living room is the training ground. The hallway at school is the battlefield.

Set aside time to role-play specific scenarios with your child. You play the friend. They play themselves. Keep it realistic. Use the tone, the language, and the social dynamics they actually face. This will feel awkward at first, especially with older kids. Do it anyway. Awkwardness in your living room is better than freezing up when it counts.

Scenario one: the party invitation. Your child gets invited to a party where there won't be parental supervision, or where they know alcohol or other substances will be available. Here's a script they can use: "That sounds fun, but I can't make it. My parents already have something planned." Simple. No explanation needed. No moral lecture. If the friend pushes, the follow-up is: "Yeah, it's not up to me. Maybe next time." The goal is to give your child a response that closes the door without creating a confrontation. Practice this until it sounds natural coming out of their mouth.

Scenario two: inappropriate content sharing. Someone in a group chat sends an explicit image, a cruel meme about another student, or a link to something your child knows they shouldn't view. This happens constantly, and the social expectation is to laugh, share, or at least stay silent. Script: "I'm good." Two words. If pressed: "That's not really my thing." If shamed: "You do you. I'm just not into it." Coach your child that leaving a group chat where this happens regularly is also an option, and it's a strong one. They don't owe their presence to a conversation that tramples their values. Remind them that staying silent in a chat where harmful content circulates can look like agreement to anyone watching from the outside. Exiting quietly is a form of clarity that protects both their integrity and their reputation.

Scenario three: the dare or direct challenge. A friend or group directly challenges your child to do something risky. Shoplifting, sneaking out, trying a substance, sending a message they shouldn't send. Script: "Nah, I'm not doing that." Full stop. If the group pushes, uses insults, or questions their courage: "Call it whatever you want. I'm still not doing it." Practice the tone here. Steady voice, relaxed posture, no anger. You want your child to deliver these lines with the same energy they'd use when turning down a food they don't like. Casual. Firm. Done. The energy behind the words matters as much as the words themselves. If your child delivers the line while staring at the ground and fidgeting, the group reads uncertainty and pushes harder. Eye contact, a relaxed stance, and a steady voice signal that the decision is already made and there's nothing to negotiate.

Scenario four: the slow compromise. This one is trickier because it doesn't happen all at once. A friend gradually normalizes behavior that your child wouldn't have accepted six months ago. The language shifts. The humor gets darker. The activities push further. Teach your child to recognize the drift and to name it, at least to themselves: "This group is heading somewhere I don't want to go." Then give them a script for pulling back without torching the relationship: "I'm going to hang with other people for a while." They don't need to explain why or issue a moral verdict.

A critical coaching point through all of these: standing firm doesn't mean preaching. Your child's job is to hold their line, not to correct everyone else's behavior. The moment they start lecturing their friends about right and wrong, they'll be labeled and tuned out. Quiet confidence usually lands harder than a loud correction. Daniel didn't give a speech at the king's table about why the food was wrong. He simply said, "I'd rather not," and offered a reasonable alternative. Your child can follow the same principle. Living differently speaks louder than explaining why everyone else should change.

After each role-play session, debrief. Ask your child what felt hard, what felt natural, and what they'd change. Then adjust the scripts to fit their personality and their real social world. A response that works for a confident, outgoing thirteen-year-old won't always work for a quiet, introverted ten-year-old. Keep shaping the language until it sounds like something your child would actually say.

One mistake to avoid: don't script so heavily that your child sounds rehearsed. The goal is to give them a few anchor phrases and a simple structure. The specifics should flex with the moment. Think of it like learning to cook. You teach the basic technique, and then they adjust based on what's in front of them.

Finding Like-Minded Community

Resisting negative influence is only half the equation. Your child also needs to be pulled toward something good. Saying no gets exhausting when there's nothing to say yes to. That's where intentional community matters.

Help your child find peers who share their values. Youth groups, service projects, sports teams with strong leadership, and academic clubs with healthy cultures. These spaces give your child proof that they aren't the only one living by a different standard. That proof matters more than you might think. One of the strongest drivers of peer pressure is the belief that "everyone" is doing something. When your child has a circle of friends who aren't, the power of that argument weakens. The lie that "everyone does this" suddenly has a counterexample sitting next to them at lunch. Sometimes, one solid friendship is the difference between caving and holding the line.

Be proactive about this. Don't just hope your child stumbles into the right group. Look at what's available in your church, your school, and your community. If your church youth group is solid, invest in it. Drive the carpool. Host the gatherings. Make your home a place where your child's good friendships have room to grow. Stock the fridge, keep the Wi-Fi password simple, and let your living room be the gathering spot. When your home becomes the hub, you gain natural visibility into who your child spends time with and how those relationships actually work. You also send an unspoken message: this family values community enough to put time and money behind it.

As your child gets older and dating enters the picture, they'll need boundary scripts for romantic relationships, too. Teach them early: "I like spending time with you, but I'm not comfortable with that." And: "If this relationship requires me to go against what I believe, it's not the right relationship." These aren't dramatic declarations. They're calm, clear lines that protect your child's integrity when emotions make everything feel urgent.

Encourage your child to look for friends who make them stronger, not friends who require them to become weaker. Healthy friendships have a particular feel: mutual respect, honesty, room for disagreement, and encouragement toward growth. When your child can describe what a good friendship looks like, they'll recognize it when they see it, and they'll notice when something keeps falling short.

Playbook Implementation: Internal Validation Exercise

Put this chapter into practice with two specific actions.

First, start a daily identity affirmation with your child. Each morning or evening, speak one truth over them rooted in who God says they are. Keep it specific and varied. "You are chosen and deeply loved" (Colossians 3:12). "God made you with purpose, and that purpose doesn't depend on what anyone at school thinks." Over time, these truths become the internal voice that pushes back against external pressure. Write a few on index cards and rotate them through the week so the words stay fresh.

Second, schedule a peer pressure practice session this week. Pick two of the scenarios from this chapter and role-play them at the dinner table or during a car ride. Let your child practice their responses out loud. Swap roles so they can also feel what it's like to be the one applying pressure. This builds empathy and sharpens their ability to recognize tactics when they're on the receiving end. Aim for ten to fifteen minutes, keep it light, and repeat it monthly. The more familiar these moments feel in practice, the less power they'll hold in real life.

5

DECISION-MAKING TRAINING: TEACHING KIDS TO THINK, NOT JUST OBEY

Your twelve-year-old daughter is standing in the kitchen doorway, arms crossed, waiting for your answer. Her friend's older sister is driving a group to the mall on Saturday, and she wants to go. You've never met the older sister. You don't know how long she's had her license. And the group includes a couple of kids whose names you've only heard in passing. Every instinct in you wants to say no, shut it down, and get back to dinner.

But she will face this exact moment hundreds of times over the next several years, and you will not always be in the kitchen when it happens. So the question is not whether she goes to the mall this Saturday. It's whether she has the inner tools to size up a situation, weigh what matters, and make a wise call when you're nowhere in sight.

Most Christian parents do an excellent job teaching their kids what to believe. Fewer spend the same energy teaching them how to think. There's a real difference between a child who obeys because you said so and a child who chooses well because they've learned how to evaluate options through wisdom, safety, and faith. The first child needs you in the room. The second carries that skill with them.

This chapter gives you a practical system for building that second kind of child.

The Street-Smart Decision Framework

Proverbs 14:15 says, "The simple believe anything, but the prudent give thought to their steps." That verse captures the aim of decision-making training. You are raising a child who thinks about their steps before they take them. You're helping them become someone who filters choices through wisdom instead of impulse, emotion, or the pull of the crowd.

The Street-Smart Decision Framework is a simple, repeatable tool your child can use in almost any situation. Picture it as a mental checklist they can run in thirty seconds, whether they're at a party, on a group chat, or standing in a parking lot deciding whether to get in someone's car. It has four steps, and each one builds on the last.

Step One: Stop and Name It. Before your child does anything, they need to notice that a decision is in front of them. That sounds obvious, yet a lot of bad choices happen because kids never register that they're choosing at all. They just go along with whatever is happening. Train your child to spot decision moments: "Someone just offered me something." "The group is heading somewhere I wasn't expecting." "I feel pressure to say yes." Once they can name what's happening, they've already stepped off autopilot.

Step Two: Check the Cost. This is a risk assessment. Teach your child to ask one direct question: "What could go wrong, and can I live with that?" For a ten-year-old, that might sound like, "If I post this mean thing about my friend, what happens tomorrow at school?" For a fourteen-year-old, it gets more serious: "If I ride with this person and something goes wrong, what's at risk?" You're training them to look past the moment and notice the second and third consequences sitting behind the decision.

One practical way to teach consequence thinking is to use what-then chains at the dinner table. Pick a scenario and walk it through together.

"What if you copied answers from a friend on the test? Then what? The teacher might catch it. Then what? You'd get a zero and a call home. Then what? Your grade drops, and your trust with us takes a hit." Do this often enough, and your child starts running those chains on their own, in real time.

Step Three: Check the Standard. This is where biblical wisdom gets practical. Your child asks, "Does this line up with what I know is right?" You're not asking them to recite a verse under pressure. You're asking them to measure the choice against the values your family has already taught and practiced: honesty, respect, safety, and integrity. If the action contradicts those values, that is a clear signal to step back, even if the pull is strong.

Step Four: Decide and Own It. The final step is action. Your child makes the call and takes responsibility for it. This matters. You want them to feel the weight of their choices, good and bad, because ownership is what turns experience into wisdom. A child who blames friends, the situation, or bad luck will repeat the same mistakes. A child who can say, "I chose this, and here's why," is building self-awareness that will protect them for years.

To introduce the framework, pick a calm, low-pressure moment. Walk your child through the four steps using a recent decision they've already made, something small and safe. Maybe they skipped basketball practice to hang out with a friend, or they spent their birthday money right away instead of saving it. Run that choice through the steps together. Because it's already behind them, the conversation feels like training, not discipline.

Repetition is the point. You want the steps to become so familiar that your child uses them without even naming them. Like a basketball player who shoots free throws until the motion is natural, your child should be able to move through Stop, Cost, Standard, and Own It quickly and clearly.

Guided Practice Opportunities

A framework only helps if your child actually uses it. The best way to prepare them for high-stakes moments is to give them low-stakes practice as often as you can. That means your everyday family life becomes the training ground: real decisions, real outcomes, and growing confidence.

Start with age-appropriate choices that have genuine consequences, but manageable ones. For kids ages eight to ten, that might look like letting them decide how to spend a small weekly allowance, choose between two weekend activities, or handle a minor conflict with a sibling before you step in. The choice has to be real. If you're going to overrule them every time, you're not training them. You're putting on a show.

With tweens, eleven to thirteen, raise the stakes a bit. Let them plan part of the grocery list within a budget. Give them a say in how after-school time is structured, inside boundaries you've already set. If they want to attend a friend's event, have them present their case: who will be there, what time it ends, how they'll get home, and why they think it's a good use of their time. You're not interrogating them. You're teaching them to think through logistics and accountability before they ask for a yes.

Here is a scenario you can use this week. Tell your thirteen-year-old, "You have sixty dollars from your birthday. You can spend it, save it, or split it. You decide, but walk me through your thinking." Then listen. If they say, "I want to buy a new video game," ask them to run it through the framework. What's the cost? They'll have zero dollars left. Does it line up with what they value? Maybe yes, maybe no. Are they owning the choice? They should be. Then, when the money is gone, and they spot something else they want two weeks later, the lesson lands. You did not lecture. The consequence taught.

For teenagers, fourteen and up, practice needs to include social pressure. Role-play is one of the best tools here, even though your teen may roll their eyes at first. (I have yet to meet a teen who loved role-play on the first try.) Set up a situation: "Your friend just texted and wants you to sneak out to meet a group at the park at midnight. What do you do?" Let your teen talk it through. If they say, "I'd just say no," go further. "How would you say no?" "What if they call you scared?" "What if they say everyone's going?" The point is to make the pressure feel familiar in a safe setting, so they have words ready when it counts.

You can also use current events and real stories as practice material. When you hear about a teenager in the news for a poor choice, pause and ask, "Where do you think the decision went wrong? What would the framework have looked like for that person?" It lowers defensiveness and helps your child practice clear thinking on someone else's situation. Over time, they'll start doing the same with their own choices.

Confidence grows when kids see a good decision pay off. When your daughter saves half her money and has enough to buy something she really wants a month later, name it: "That was a solid call. You thought it through." When your son sits out a group prank and later learns the other kids got in trouble, point it out without gloating: "Your judgment was right. That's worth trusting." Those small wins add up. Over time, your child trusts their own judgment because they've watched it work.

A few scripts to use during practice moments:

"Walk me through your thinking on this."

"What's the best thing that could happen? What's the worst?"

"If you make this choice and it doesn't go well, what's your plan?"

"I trust you to decide this. I just want to hear how you're weighing it."

These phrases do something important: they tell your child you believe they're capable of thinking, and you expect them to do it. You're staying in the coach role, not acting like a referee who blows the whistle on every play.

The Wrong Choice Recovery System

Your child will make bad decisions. Guaranteed. What you do next matters as much as anything, because recovery is where a lot of wisdom gets built.

Most parents default to one of two extremes. Some come down hard with heavy punishment, long lectures, and a withdrawal of trust that drags on for weeks. Others minimize it, brush it off with a quick "just don't do it again," and move on without any real process. Both miss the point. The first teaches your child to hide failures. The second teaches them that failures do not matter. Neither builds wisdom.

The Wrong Choice Recovery System has three steps: Acknowledge, Assess, and Rebuild.

Acknowledge means your child names what happened honestly, without excuses. You set the tone. If you come in heated, they'll shut down and start defending themselves. If you come in calm and direct, honesty is more likely. Try this: "Tell me what happened, in your words." Then listen, all the way through. Don't interrupt. Don't correct. Let them talk. When they're done, reflect on what you heard: "So you went along with the group even though you felt uneasy about it." That is acknowledgment without shame. You're helping them see the choice clearly without burying them in guilt.

Assess means walking through the decision together using the framework. Where did the process break down? Did they skip "check the cost"? Did they notice it was a decision moment and ignore the signal? Did peer pressure override what they already knew was right? Keep this step analytical, not emotional. Treat it like game film. A coach does not help a player by screaming about a missed tackle. A good coach rewinds the play and points out what went wrong so it can be fixed next time.

Try: "Let's walk through this together. Where do you think it went sideways?" Or: "If you could rewind to the moment right before you decided, what would you do differently?" Those questions keep the conversation moving forward and put your child in the driver's seat of their own growth.

Rebuild is where trust gets restored. This is the step many families skip, and it's often the most important. Your child needs a clear, specific path back. If trust was broken, spell out what rebuilding looks like: "For the next two weeks, I need you to check in with me when you get to your friend's house. After that, we'll reassess." This is not vague punishment. It has a timeline and a goal. Your child can see the finish line, which gives them something concrete to work toward.

Restoration also includes spiritual repair. Pray with your child. Keep it brief and sincere, not long and heavy. "God, thank You that we can learn from this. Help us both grow wiser. Amen." You're showing them that failure is part of being human and that God's grace meets us in the middle of our worst moments, not only after we've cleaned ourselves up.

A common mistake is holding onto disappointment long after the recovery work is done. If your child has acknowledged what happened, assessed what went wrong, and rebuilt trust through the steps you set, release it. Bringing up old failures in future arguments wrecks the trust you're trying to rebuild. It teaches your child that forgiveness comes with strings attached, and that's not the gospel.

Advanced Discernment Training

Once your child knows the decision-making framework and has used it in daily life, you can add deeper discernment skills. These are the skills that protect them when the right choice isn't obvious, when the danger is subtle, and when everyone around them acts like everything is fine.

Start with situational awareness. Teach your child to read a room. Who seems to be in charge? What's the mood? Is anything making me uncomfortable, even if I can't explain why? That quiet sense that something is off is worth paying attention to. Proverbs 27:12 puts it plainly: "The prudent see danger and take refuge, but the simple keep going and pay the penalty." Train your child to trust that internal signal and act on it, even if they cannot explain it in the moment. They can explain later. First, get to safety.

Next, teach them to evaluate people with clear eyes. That does not mean becoming suspicious of everyone. It means watching what people do over time, not just what they say in the moment. Ask your child, "Does this person treat others well when nobody important is watching?" "Do they keep their word?" "Do they respect boundaries when it costs them something?" Those are markers of character. When your child learns to spot them, they'll start moving toward the right people and backing away from the wrong ones with less need for you to step in.

Strategic thinking is the final layer. This is where you help your child zoom out and consider longer-term consequences. A fourteen-year-old sending an angry text might feel justified, but that text stays on a screen. A twelve-year-old posting a photo to impress friends may not realize how easily it spreads. Help your child connect today's choices to tomorrow's outcomes: "What does this look like in a week? In a year?" Thinking in longer time frames is a skill many adults struggle with, so giving your child practice now puts them ahead.

Playbook Implementation: Decision-Making Practice Lab

Put this into action this week with two specific exercises.

Weekly Decision Scenario. Once a week, at dinner or during a car ride, give your child a realistic scenario: "You're at a sleepover, and your friend's older brother offers everyone a sip of beer. What do you do?" Walk through the four-step framework together. Rotate between social pressure, money decisions, online situations, and safety calls. Keep it relaxed. You're training their thinking, not trying to catch them.

Family Decision Evaluation Rubric. When a family decision comes up, whether it's choosing a vacation spot, setting a new rule, or handling a scheduling conflict, bring your child into the process. Use this simple rubric together: What are our options? What's the potential cost of each one? Which option lines up best with our family values? Who owns the final call, and why? Write the rubric on a notecard and keep it on the fridge. (I keep a stack of blank notecards in a kitchen drawer for things like this.) The more your child sees the process in real life, the more natural it feels when they're on their own.

Both exercises take less than ten minutes. Skip the perfectionism here. Do it, keep it moving, and let the consistency do the work.

6

DIGITAL DISCIPLESHIP: NAVIGATING SCREENS AND SOCIAL MEDIA

Your ten-year-old is sitting on the couch, tablet propped on his knees, headphones on, zoned out. You glance at the screen as you walk by and catch a flash of something you weren't expecting. Maybe it's a YouTube video with language you'd never allow at the dinner table. Maybe it's a group chat where kids are roasting each other with a cruelty that makes your stomach turn. Or maybe it's the sixth straight hour of mindless scrolling on a Saturday, and you realize your kid hasn't spoken a full sentence to another human being since breakfast. That familiar knot shows up in your chest. You want to grab the device and toss it in the trash, but you also know that move will explode into a two-hour standoff. So you do nothing. You walk past, tell yourself you'll deal with it later, and the knot stays right where it is.

That moment is more common than most parents admit. The tension behind it is real: you know screens are shaping your child's thinking, but you don't have a clear system for managing them. You're winging it. Some days you're strict. Some days you're lenient. The inconsistency eats away at your authority, and your child senses the gap and uses it the way any smart kid would.

The core problem goes deeper than screen time limits. Most families have screens without a philosophy. They have devices in the home without a shared understanding of why those devices exist, what they're for, and what boundaries protect the people using them. Without that foundation, every screen-related conversation turns into a negotiation, and negotiations with a determined eleven-year-old rarely end well.

This chapter lays out a complete system. You'll start by building a biblical media philosophy, then add practical boundaries, content evaluation skills, and a device-management approach that keeps your household steadier. By the end, you'll have a working family digital contract you can customize and use this week.

Biblical Media Philosophy Foundation

Before you set a single rule about screen time, settle this for yourself: what does God's Word actually say about what we take in through our eyes and ears? If your media rules are built only on fear or frustration, your kids will see through them fast. Rules without reasons create rebels. Rules anchored to clear biblical principles give kids something they can eventually carry on their own.

Philippians 4:8 gives one of the clearest filters in Scripture: "Whatever is true, whatever is noble, whatever is right, whatever is pure, whatever is lovely, whatever is admirable, if anything is excellent or praiseworthy, think about such things." Paul wrote that to adults living in a Roman culture overflowing with entertainment, spectacle, and moral compromise. The instruction wasn't "avoid all culture." It was "choose wisely what occupies your mind." That distinction matters. You're raising kids to be discerning participants in their world, and discernment starts with a standard for what gets access to their attention.

Proverbs 4:23 adds another layer: "Above all else, guard your heart, for everything you do flows from it." The heart, in biblical terms, is the seat of your child's beliefs, desires, and motivations. What they watch, read, scroll through, and listen to feeds directly into that space. You wouldn't let a stranger walk into your home and whisper into your child's ear for three hours a day. Yet that's functionally what unfiltered media access does. The stranger just happens to be an algorithm built to hold attention at all costs.

Here's how to translate that into a working family philosophy. Sit down with your kids and explain two simple ideas. First: our family believes that what goes into our minds shapes who we become. Second: because of that, we choose carefully what we give our attention to. Frame it in age-appropriate ways. For an eight-year-old, you might say, "Your brain is like a garden. What you watch and listen to plants seeds. We want to plant good ones." For a twelve-year-old, you can be more direct: "The stuff you scroll through every day trains your brain to think a certain way. We're going to be intentional about that, because your mind matters too much to hand it over to whoever shows up in your feed."

That philosophy becomes the why behind every rule you set. When your child asks, "Why can't I have TikTok?" you have an answer rooted in something bigger than "because I said so." You can say, "Our family guards what goes into our minds because we believe what you think about shapes who you become. That app feeds you content based on what holds your attention the longest, and a lot of it doesn't pass our family's filter." That's a conversation, not a command. Conversations build the kind of internal filter that still works when your child isn't under your roof.

One common mistake is treating all media as equally dangerous. It's tempting to lump everything together and go full lockdown. But a child watching a well-made nature documentary and a child scrolling anonymous social media feeds at midnight are having two completely different experiences. Your philosophy should help your kids see that difference. Teach them to evaluate content against a simple standard: Does this build me up or tear me down? Does this point me toward the truth or pull me away from it? Does this honor the way God made people, or does it mock and degrade them? Those questions travel well. Your child can carry them into any media situation, with or without you in the room.

The goal of a biblical media philosophy is to move your child from external compliance to internal conviction. You won't always be standing over their shoulder. At some point, they'll be at a friend's house, they'll have their own phone, or they'll be in a dorm room with zero parental oversight. The real question is whether they'll have a working filter by then. Building that filter starts now, and it starts with a clear why rooted in Scripture and explained in plain language your child actually understands.

The Screen Boundary System

Philosophy without structure is just a nice idea. You need boundaries, and those boundaries need to be clear enough that everyone in the house knows what's expected. Vague rules like "don't spend too much time on screens" fall apart because "too much" means something different to every person in the family. Your child will always interpret it more generously than you do. So get specific.

Start with platform guidelines based on your child's age. For kids ages eight to ten, the simplest approach is shared-device-only access. They use a family tablet or computer in a common area. There's no personal phone, no personal social media accounts, and no unsupervised Internet browsing. The apps on the device are ones you've chosen and reviewed. At this age, your child doesn't need access to YouTube's open platform. YouTube Kids or a curated playlist you build yourself gives them plenty of content without the algorithmic rabbit holes that lead to increasingly extreme or inappropriate material.

For kids ages eleven to thirteen, you can introduce a little more freedom while keeping strong guardrails. If you decide to give them a phone, consider starting with a basic phone or a managed smartphone with heavy parental controls. Apps like Bark, Qustodio, or built-in Apple Screen Time and Google Family Link let you approve or block specific apps, set daily time limits, and monitor activity without reading every single text message. Social media at this age is a case-by-case decision, and most families are better off delaying it. If you allow any platform, require full access to the account, including the password and the ability to check messages.

For kids ages fourteen and fifteen, the leash gets longer, but it doesn't disappear. You can allow more independent app use and possibly a social media account, but only with a clear agreement in place. They know you have access. They know you'll check periodically. They also understand that trust is earned through consistent behavior, not demanded through arguments.

Now, time limits. What actually works is specific, predictable windows rather than floating daily totals. Telling a child "you get two hours of screen time today" invites constant negotiation about when those hours happen and what counts. A better approach is to designate screen time blocks. For example, screens are available from 4:00 to 5:30 on school days, and from 9:00 to 11:00 on Saturday mornings. Outside those windows, devices are off and put away. That removes the negotiation because the schedule is the schedule. It's the same reason bedtime works better than "go to bed when you're tired."

Where devices live matters as much as when they're used; establish device-free zones in your home. Bedrooms and the dinner table are the two most important ones. Devices charge overnight in a common area, like the kitchen counter. If you need a place to start, the kitchen counter is my go-to because it's visible and hard to ignore when everyone walks by. This one rule eliminates most late-night scrolling, secret social media use, and exposure to content your child isn't ready for. If the phone sleeps in your child's room, you're trusting a ten-year-old to exercise more self-control than most adults manage. Move the charger. It's one of the simplest, most effective boundaries you can set.

Supervision doesn't have to feel like surveillance. Frame it as involvement rather than suspicion. Sit with your younger kids while they watch. Ask your older kids what they're watching or playing and actually listen to the answer. Play a round of their favorite game with them. When you show real interest, you're communicating that their digital world matters to you, and you're also keeping a pulse on what's coming through the screen. A child who knows their parent is engaged is far less likely to chase content they'd be embarrassed to share.

One practical tip that often gets overlooked is a "screen sabbath." Pick one day a week, or even half a day, when the whole family goes screen-free. Everyone, parents included. It resets your baseline. It also removes the double standard kids spot instantly: "You tell me to get off my phone, but you're on yours all the time." If you're going to ask them to do it, you have to do it too.

Critical Evaluation of Content

Boundaries control access. Discernment shapes the mind. You need both, but the second one is what lasts. Your child will eventually be in situations where no parental filter exists. They need an internal filter that kicks in on its own when they run into content that clashes with their values.

Teaching kids to analyze secular messaging starts with this: every piece of media carries a message. Nothing is neutral. A TV show communicates values through which characters are celebrated and which are mocked. A song normalizes a certain view of relationships, money, or identity. A social media trend reinforces what's "cool" and what's "weird." Your child absorbs these messages whether they realize it or not. Your job is to bring that process into the open so they can see it happening.

Start with a simple exercise you can do during any show, movie, or video you watch together. Ask three questions: What is this trying to tell me is true? What is this saying matters most? Does that line up with what our family believes? You don't need to turn every movie night into a theology class. Just drop one question casually during or after the show. "What do you think that character cares about most?" "Do you agree with how they handled that situation?" Low-pressure questions like these train your child's brain to process media actively instead of passively.

As your child gets older, you can talk about worldview conflicts more directly. Every piece of content is built on assumptions about what's real, what's good, and what makes life meaningful. Some of those assumptions line up with a biblical worldview, and some push hard in the opposite direction. A popular show might say following your feelings is always the right choice. Another might treat authority figures as corrupt by default and not worth listening to. Others suggest identity is something you invent with no reference point outside your own desires. Your child doesn't need to reject every show that contains a competing idea. They do need to recognize the idea and test it against what they know to be true.

Here's a script you can use with a child around age ten or eleven: "Everything you watch is trying to teach you something, even when it doesn't look like a lesson. Our job is to pay attention to what it's teaching and decide if it's true. Some of it will be great. Some of it will be off. You get to be the one who decides, and I'll help you think it through."

For older kids, around twelve to fifteen, you can go further: "The people who create content have a perspective on how life works. Sometimes that perspective lines up with ours, sometimes it doesn't. I want you to be smart enough to tell the difference. That's a skill, and we're going to practice it together."

The goal is to build a three-question content filter that your child carries with them. When they encounter any media, they instinctively ask: Is this true? Is this helpful? Is this honoring to God and to people? Over time, this becomes automatic. They don't need you hovering over their shoulder because they've internalized a standard that operates on its own. That's the difference between a child who avoids bad content because they'll get in trouble and a child who avoids it because they recognize it for what it is.

A common mistake parents make here is critiquing secular media while giving "Christian" media a free pass. Some content labeled as Christian is poorly made, theologically shallow, or emotionally manipulative. Teach your child to apply the same filter to everything. Truth is truth regardless of the label on the packaging, and weak thinking dressed in Christian language is still weak thinking.

Device Management Without World War III

You've set boundaries. You've built a philosophy. Now comes the part every parent dreads: enforcing it when your child pushes back. Because they will. The twelve-year-old who was fine with the rules last month suddenly insists every friend has unlimited access and you're ruining their social life. The nine-year-old melts down when screen time ends. The fourteen-year-old finds a workaround you didn't even know existed. This is normal. How you respond in these moments determines whether your system holds or starts to collapse.

Start here: take devices calmly. The biggest escalation trigger in screen conflict is a parent who grabs a device in anger. The moment you snatch a phone or slam a laptop shut, you've turned a boundary into a battle. Use a calm, matter-of-fact approach instead. Walk up, make eye contact, and say, "Screen time is done for today. Please hand me the tablet." If they protest, repeat the instruction once without raising your voice: "I hear you. Screen time is still done. Hand it over, please." If they refuse, don't wrestle for it. State the consequence: "If the tablet isn't in my hand in the next thirty seconds, you'll lose screen time tomorrow as well." Then wait. Silence helps. Most kids will comply when they see you're calm and serious.

Here are a few more scripts for common situations:

"I know you want to keep playing. The time we agreed on is up, and I need the controller now."

"Your screen time privilege depends on following the schedule. When you hand it over without a fight, you're showing me you can handle the responsibility."

"I checked your phone and found something that doesn't match our family agreement. We're going to talk about it after dinner, and your phone stays with me until then."

Notice the pattern in each of these: you state the situation, you state what you need, and you connect it to either the agreement or a consequence. No yelling. No lecturing. No extended debate. Brevity is power.

Building cooperation around screen time works better when your child is involved from the start. When kids feel rules are imposed without any input, they resist harder. When they've had a voice in setting boundaries, they're more likely to respect them. This doesn't mean your child gets veto power. It means you sit down together, explain the system, ask for input on things like which time window works best, and let them feel some ownership over the schedule. "We need to set screen time boundaries. Here's what I'm thinking. What would work best for you within these guidelines?" That small act of inclusion reduces conflict.

Consequences for digital boundary violations should be clear, consistent, and directly related to the offense. If your child sneaks screen time after hours, they lose the next day's screen time. If they download an app without permission, the phone goes to a basic phone setup for a week. If they're caught on a platform they've been told to avoid, they lose the device entirely for a set period. The key is following through every time. One free pass teaches your child that the rules are suggestions. Consistent enforcement teaches them the rules are real.

One thing to watch for: don't make screen removal the default punishment for every unrelated offense. If your child doesn't clean their room, taking their phone away doesn't teach them responsibility for their space. Reserve digital consequences for digital violations. That keeps the connection between behavior and outcome clear, which is what makes consequences effective in the first place.

Playbook Implementation: Family Digital Contract

Everything from this chapter comes together in one document: your family digital contract. This is a written agreement between you and your child that spells out expectations, privileges, and consequences around screens and devices. Writing it down removes ambiguity and gives everyone a reference point when disagreements show up.

Your contract should cover five areas: approved devices and platforms, screen time schedule, device-free zones and charging rules, content standards, and consequences for violations. Sit down with your child and fill it out together. Let them see that you're holding yourself to the same standards where it applies. If the dinner table is device-free, your phone goes away too. If there's a screen sabbath, you participate. That shared accountability keeps the contract from feeling like restrictions aimed at one person.

Build in a regular review. Once a month, sit down for fifteen minutes and evaluate how the system is working. Ask your child what feels fair and what feels too tight. Share what you've noticed. Adjust where it makes sense without abandoning the core principles. This review process teaches your child that rules can be reasonable and that maturity is rewarded with increased freedom.

That leads to the most important piece: age-progression planning. Your contract at age eight should look different from your contract at twelve, and both should look different from your contract at fifteen. Map out, even roughly, what increased freedoms look like at each stage. When your child sees a clear path toward more independence, they're motivated to show the responsibility that earns it. "When you've shown me six months of following our current agreement, we'll talk about adding this app." That's concrete and motivating. It turns digital discipleship from a series of restrictions into a training plan that prepares your child to manage media wisely.

This week, draft your first version of the contract. Keep it simple. One page. Review it together as a family this weekend, then put it somewhere obvious. It doesn't need to be perfect. It needs to be clear enough that you can point to it when the same argument shows up again next Tuesday.

7

THE MASTER SCRIPTS: COMMUNICATION FRAMEWORK FOR HEAVY TOPICS

Your eleven-year-old climbs into the car after school, drops her backpack on the floor, and stares out the window. You ask how her day went. Fine. You ask what happened at lunch. Nothing. Then, three miles from home, she says it: "Mom, a kid in my class says Christians hate gay people. Is that true?" Your hands tighten on the steering wheel. Your mind races through fifteen possible responses. You can feel the weight of it, the sense that whatever comes out of your mouth in the next ten seconds could shape how your daughter sees her faith, her friendships, and her God.

Every parent hits moments like this. The question lands without warning, and it demands more than a pat answer. The problem is that most of us were never given a framework for these conversations. We grew up in an era where parents could say, "Because I said so," or "The Bible says it's wrong," and that was enough. Today, your kids are processing cultural debates in real time, comparing your answers against what they hear from teachers, influencers, and peers. A vague or panicked response doesn't just miss the mark. It teaches your child that these topics are off-limits at home, which means they'll go looking for answers somewhere else.

This chapter gives you a communication system. You'll walk away with a clear framework for any difficult topic, ready-to-use scripts for the conversations that keep parents up at night, and a method for teaching your kids to hold their own in tough discussions with grace and confidence.

The Master Communication Framework

Most effective hard conversations follow a pattern. Once you see it, you can use it for almost anything, from politics to pornography. Think of it like a play design in football. You don't run a brand-new scheme for every single play. You have a core structure that adjusts to the situation.

Here's the framework, built on four moves: **Listen, Anchor, Guide, Equip.**

Listen first. When your child brings up a hard question, your first job is to hear what's actually being asked. A ten-year-old asking, "What does transgender mean?" is usually asking a very different question than the cultural debate you're picturing in your head. Pause. Take a breath. Then say something like, "That's a really good question. Tell me more about what made you think about this." You're doing two things at once: buying yourself thirty seconds to think and gathering information about what your child actually needs. A lot of the time, kids are trying to make sense of something a friend said, something they saw on a screen, or a feeling they can't name yet. The question behind the question matters more than the words they used.

Anchor in truth. Once you understand what's really being asked, ground your response in a biblical principle. Keep it simple and practical. You don't need to deliver a theology lecture. One clear anchoring statement is enough: "God made every person with value and purpose," or "In our family, we believe God's design for [topic] is..." This gives your child a reference point. It's the fixed point they can return to as the conversation gets more complicated.

Guide with honesty. This is where you share age-appropriate information. The key phrase is *age-appropriate,* and it's worth slowing down for a second to define it. For kids ages six to nine, stick with broad truths and simple language. They need categories, not details. For ten to twelve, you can add complexity, acknowledge that people disagree, and explain why your family holds its position. For those thirteen and up, treat them more like young adults. Give them the fuller picture, including the strongest arguments on the other side, and help them think through why you believe what you believe. The goal is progressive honesty. You share a little more each year, matching the information to their ability to process it.

A practical test: if your answer would confuse a child that age, you've gone too deep. If it would insult the intelligence of a child that age, you haven't gone deep enough.

Equip for the next conversation. Every hard topic will come up again, in a different form, with a different friend, in a different classroom. So end each conversation by giving your child something portable: a phrase they can use, a way to think about the issue, or a question they can ask themselves when it surfaces later. "When someone brings this up at school, you can say, 'My family sees it differently, and I respect that we don't all agree.'" That turns a one-time talk into something they can actually carry with them.

Creating a safe space for honest questions means your reaction matters as much as your answer. If you gasp, lecture, or shut down the first time your child brings up something uncomfortable, they learn fast: don't ask Mom or Dad. You want to be the first resource, which means your face, your tone, and your body language need to say *I'm glad you brought this to me* even when your insides are doing backflips. One father I know made a house rule: "You can ask us anything, and you'll never get in trouble for asking." His kids tested it. They asked about things that made him squirm. Over time, though, they came to him with everything because they knew the door stayed open. That's the kind of culture you're building.

Scripts for Cultural and Current Events

Cultural and political controversies will reach your child whether you're ready or not. The goal is to give them a framework before the world hands them a storyline. Let's work through three of the most common scenarios.

Discussing political and social issues biblically. Your twelve-year-old comes home and says, "My teacher says we should all support [political cause]. Are we supposed to?" This is a training moment. Fight the urge to rant about the teacher or the cause. Instead, walk through the Listen, Anchor, Guide, Equip framework.

Try this: "It sounds like your teacher feels strongly about that. What did you think when you heard it?" Let your child talk. Then anchor: "In our family, we look at issues through what the Bible teaches about how God wants us to treat people and live in the world. Sometimes that lines up with one side, sometimes the other, and sometimes neither." Then guide: "On this particular issue, here's what we believe and why..." Keep your explanation clear and specific to your family's convictions. Then equip: "If your teacher or a friend asks what you think, you can say, 'I'm still learning about this, and my family has some thoughts I'm working through.' You don't have to have a perfect answer on the spot."

The key principle here comes from Romans 14, where Paul addresses disputable matters. Some issues have clear biblical positions. Others are areas where faithful Christians disagree. Teaching your child to tell the difference is one of the most valuable skills you can give them. When the Bible speaks clearly, your family can speak clearly. When it's an area of wisdom and conviction rather than direct command, you model thoughtfulness instead of swagger.

Responding to school curriculum conflicts. Maybe your child's health class presents material that conflicts with your values. Maybe a literature assignment includes content you find inappropriate. The temptation is to either pull your child from the class or fire off an angry email.

Both might be warranted in extreme cases, but the better first move is usually to equip your child to think.

Try this conversation: "I know you're covering [topic] in class this week. Some of what you'll hear lines up with what we believe, and some of it doesn't. I want you to listen, learn, and pay attention to what feels different from what we've taught you at home. Then let's talk about it after." This approach does something important: it treats your child as a thinker, not someone who needs to be shielded from every competing idea. You're saying, "I trust your foundation enough to let you hear other perspectives and process them with me."

After the class or assignment, follow up: "What stood out to you? Was there anything that didn't sit right?" Then use that as your opening to talk through the specific points of disagreement. That discernment muscle will matter later.

Having LGBTQ and gender identity conversations. This is the one that makes most Christian parents freeze. Your child will encounter friends, classmates, teachers, or media figures who identify as LGBTQ. Pretending otherwise doesn't prepare them. Here's how to handle it with both conviction and compassion.

When your child says, "My friend told me she likes girls," or "A kid at school says they're nonbinary," start with Listen: "Thanks for telling me that. How do you feel about what your friend shared?" Let your child name their reaction. Then Anchor: "We believe God designed men and women with purpose, and that His design for relationships and identity is good. That's our foundation." Guide: "Your friend is trying to figure out who they are, and that can feel big and confusing. We can disagree with someone's beliefs or choices and still treat them with real kindness. Those two things don't cancel each other out." Equip: "If someone asks you what you think, you can say, 'I care about you, and my family has beliefs that are important to us.' You don't owe anyone a debate, and you don't have to be mean to be honest."

The biggest mistake parents make here is framing LGBTQ topics as an "us versus them" war. Your child needs to see real people, not political categories. First Peter 3:15 says to give an answer for the hope you have, but to do it with gentleness and respect. That's the standard. Your child can hold firm convictions and still be someone others feel safe around.

The Big Three: Sex, Drugs, and Violence

These three topics have always been heavy. What's changed is the age at which your children bump into them. A lot of kids see pornography for the first time somewhere between 11 and 13, and some run into it as early as elementary school. Conversations about substances are happening in school hallways long before high school. And violent content, both fictional and real, is a tap away on any device. Waiting until high school to address these topics means arriving years too late.

Age-appropriate sexuality education from a biblical perspective. The word "sex" makes many Christian parents want to hand the whole conversation off to a youth pastor or a curriculum kit. But your child needs to hear about God's design for sexuality from you, in your voice, inside the safety of your relationship.

For ages six to nine, the conversation is about bodies, boundaries, and the basics of God's design. "God made boys and girls different on purpose, and every part of your body has value. No one should touch your private areas, and you can always tell us if something makes you uncomfortable." Simple. Clear. Protective.

For ages ten to twelve, the conversation expands. "Sex is something God created for marriage between a husband and wife. It's a good thing in the right context. You're going to hear about it from friends and online, and some of what you hear will be wrong or incomplete. I want to be the person you come to with questions." At this age, you also need to address pornography directly: "There are images and videos online that show sex in a way that's harmful and nothing like what God intended. If you ever see something like that, and you probably will, come tell us. You won't be in trouble. We just want to help you process it."

For ages thirteen and up, go deeper. Talk about consent, emotional readiness, the difference between love and lust, and the messages they're getting about hooking up, dating apps, and body image. Ground every point in the principle that sexuality reflects God's design for intimacy, commitment, and trust within marriage. "The world says sex is casual. We believe it's significant. Here's why that matters for your future relationships."

Throughout every age, one phrase stays constant: "You can ask me anything." Repeat it. Live it. Mean it.

Substance abuse prevention conversations. "Just say no" was a great slogan, but it doesn't hold up when your twelve-year-old's best friend offers them a vape in the school bathroom. Prevention conversations need to be specific and realistic.

Start early with the concept: "Some substances change how your brain works, and your brain is still growing. We protect what matters." As your child gets older, get specific about what they'll actually run into: alcohol at parties, vaping at school, edibles that look like candy, and the pressure to try it "just once."

A strong script for your child: "Someone's going to offer you something at some point. When that happens, you've already made your decision. You don't need to decide in the moment. The decision is made. You can say, 'I'm good,' and move on. Most kids won't push back if you say it with confidence."

Help them practice the exit, too. "If you're ever at a place where things go sideways, call us. No questions asked in that moment. We will come get you." This is a safety net. It means your child has a way out that doesn't require them to explain themselves to peers in real time. Proverbs 4:23 says to guard your heart, because everything flows from it. For your child, that includes guarding their developing brain and body from substances that can change how they think and feel.

Addressing media violence and real-world safety. Your child will see violent content. Video games, movies, news footage, social media clips. The question is whether they have a filter for processing it.

When your child encounters violence in media, use it as a teaching moment: "What you just saw was designed to be exciting or shocking. Real violence looks different. It causes real pain and real loss. How did that scene make you feel?" You're training them to be a critical viewer, someone who evaluates what they consume instead of absorbing it passively.

For real-world safety conversations, particularly around school safety and community violence, be honest without creating fear: "Sad and scary things happen sometimes. We take precautions because we're wise, and we trust God because He's with us even in hard situations. If you ever feel unsafe at school or anywhere, here's exactly what I want you to do." Give them a specific plan. Identify a trusted adult at school. Establish a code word for pickup. Make it concrete.

The mistake many parents make is assuming that media violence is harmless. Psychologist Craig Anderson and other researchers have argued that heavy, repeated exposure can dull empathy and make aggression feel more normal, especially in younger kids, even as the details of how strong that effect is are still debated. Limiting exposure matters, and so does talking through what they do encounter. Psalm 101:3 says, "I will set before my eyes no worthless thing." Teaching your child to make that choice with discernment, rather than rigid rules alone, builds a lasting internal filter.

Teaching Kids to Lead Conversations

So far, the framework has focused on conversations between you and your child. Now it shifts to what happens when you're not in the room because the hardest conversations your kids will have about faith and values won't happen at the dinner table. They'll happen in the cafeteria, the group chat, and the locker room.

Sharing values respectfully. The first thing your child needs to know is that they don't have to win arguments. Their goal in peer conversations is clarity, not conquest. "You don't need to convince anyone. You just need to be honest about what you believe and why, without tearing anyone else down." That one sentence changes the whole dynamic. It takes off the pressure to perform and permits them to be straightforward.

Give your child specific phrases they can use when faith or values come up among friends:

"My family believes [X], and it's something I take seriously. I know we might see it differently."

"I respect that you think that way. Here's where I'm coming from."

"I'm still thinking through that, honestly. But right now, this is where I stand."

These phrases do three things: they state a position, they acknowledge the other person, and they close the door on a debate without slamming it. Your child stays grounded without getting combative.

Standing firm without being judgmental. This is the balance that defines a street-smart Christian kid: conviction without arrogance, firmness without harshness. Galatians 6:1 talks about restoring others in a spirit of gentleness. Your child can hold a strong position and still be the kind of friend people trust and respect.

Help them understand the difference: "Being judgmental means acting like you're better than someone because of what you believe. Standing firm means holding to your values because they matter to you, even when people disagree. You can do the second one while being kind, curious, and genuinely caring about the people around you."

Practice these conversations at home. Over dinner, at bedtime, on car rides. Throw out a scenario: "What would you say if a friend told you that all religions are the same?" Let your child practice forming a response. Coach them. Adjust their phrasing. Help them find words that feel natural, not stiff. The more they practice in safe settings, the more prepared they'll be in real ones.

One more thing: remind your child they're playing a long game. One conversation rarely changes someone's mind. But your kid will be remembered for how they talk when things get tense, and for whether they treat people like people.

Playbook Implementation: Personal Script Library

You've now seen the framework and the specific scripts. The final step is making this system yours. Every family has its own convictions, its own communication style, and its own set of topics that feel most pressing. Here's how to put it all together.

Build your script library. Take the topics covered in this chapter, plus any others specific to your family's situation, and write out your own versions of the scripts. Use the Listen, Anchor, Guide, Equip framework as your template. Keep them in a notebook, a notes app on your phone, or wherever you'll actually reference them. You don't need to memorize these word-for-word. Having the core phrases written down means you've already done the thinking before the moment arrives.

Schedule practice conversations. Set a recurring time, once a week or every two weeks, where you and your child talk through a scenario. Pick a topic from current events, something that happened at school, or a "what would you say if" situation. Keep it casual. Ten minutes is plenty. The goal is repetition. The more your child practices thinking and responding, the more natural it becomes when the real moment arrives. Think of it like a fire drill. You don't wait for the fire to figure out where the exits are.

Over time, your child will lean on the scripts less. The framework becomes instinct: listen, ground in truth, respond honestly, and leave with something they can use the next time it comes up.

8

BUILDING THE INNER CIRCLE: FRIENDS, MENTORS, AND COMMUNITY

Your twelve-year-old comes home from a weekend sleepover, and something's different. The attitude is sharper. The language is rougher around the edges. There's a new dismissiveness when you ask about school or church. You can't point to one specific thing, but your gut tells you the shift didn't come from inside your house. It came from somewhere else. Someone else.

That instinct is worth paying attention to. Because the people surrounding your child are doing one of two things at all times: reinforcing what you're building at home, or slowly pulling it apart. There's very little neutral ground. And the older your kids get, the more weight those outside voices carry.

Proverbs 13:20 puts it plainly: "Walk with the wise and become wise, for a companion of fools suffers harm." Solomon wasn't offering a suggestion. He was describing a law of influence that plays out in every cafeteria, sports team, youth group, and group chat your child enters. The people closest to your kid will shape them. Your job is to be intentional about who fills those seats.

This chapter gives you a system for evaluating, building, and protecting the relational circle around your child. Think of it as a relationship playbook: one that helps you attract the right influences, identify the wrong ones, and take specific action on both.

The Relationship Audit System

Most parents operate on a general sense of whether someone is "good" or "bad" for their child. That's a starting point, but it's too vague to be useful. A relationship audit gives you a structured way to evaluate the people who have regular access to your kid's life, so you can make clear decisions instead of reacting after the damage shows up.

Start by listing every adult and peer who has consistent, recurring contact with your child. That includes teachers, coaches, youth group leaders, friends' parents, tutors, and extended family members who spend significant time around your kids. Then look at their peers: the three to five friends your child spends the most time with, both in person and online.

For each person on that list, ask three evaluation questions. First: What values does this person model through their behavior? You're looking at actions here, not words. A coach who talks about teamwork but screams at referees is modeling something very specific. A friend's parent who jokes about underage drinking at a barbecue is sending a message your child absolutely receives, even if nobody says a word about it afterward.

Second: How does my child behave after spending time with this person? This is your most reliable data point. You might genuinely like your son's friend's dad, but if your son comes home from every visit more argumentative and disrespectful, the influence speaks for itself. Track the pattern. One off day means nothing. A consistent shift after contact with the same person is a signal you can't afford to ignore.

Third: Does this person support or undermine the standards we've set in our home? A youth leader who privately tells your daughter that your family's screen time rules are "a bit extreme" has just positioned themselves between you and your child. A teacher who mocks faith perspectives in the classroom is actively eroding something you're working to build. These moments matter more than most parents realize.

Now, let's talk about red flags in adult mentors and authority figures, because these are the influences parents tend to overlook. You naturally scrutinize your child's friends. You're less likely to question the adults. Here's what to watch for: adults who encourage secrecy from parents ("This can be just between us"), adults who consistently push boundaries you've set ("Your parents won't mind"), adults who show favorites in ways that isolate your child from their peer group, and adults who use guilt or emotional manipulation to maintain closeness with your kid.

Any one of those patterns warrants a direct conversation with that adult and, depending on the response, a restructuring of the relationship. You don't owe anyone unlimited access to your child. Full stop.

Once you've completed your audit, sort your list into three categories. Green means this person actively reinforces your family's values, and your child consistently benefits from the relationship. Yellow means this person is neutral or inconsistent, and the relationship needs monitoring. Red means this person is actively undermining your parenting or modeling behavior that contradicts your family's core standards. Red relationships need boundaries immediately. That might mean reducing contact, supervising all interactions, or ending the relationship entirely. Yellow relationships get a timeline: you watch for improvement or decline, and you move them to green or red within a set window, say sixty to ninety days.

This audit isn't something you do once and file away. Run it every three to four months, because your child's social world shifts constantly. New friendships form. Coaches change. A previously green influence can drift into yellow territory without anyone noticing unless you're paying deliberate attention.

Attracting Quality Mentors

Strong mentors don't usually show up by accident. You have to look for them with the same intentionality you'd bring to hiring someone for an important role, because that's essentially what this is. A quality mentor carries influence that either compounds what you're teaching at home or introduces something your child needs that you can't provide on your own.

The best mentors for your child share three characteristics. They live out their values consistently, meaning your child sees the same person in public and in private. They genuinely enjoy being around young people without needing to be the "cool" adult. And they naturally point your child back toward your family's authority rather than positioning themselves as an alternative to it.

Church is the obvious starting place, and it's a good one, but only if you're strategic about it. Dropping your kid off at a youth group and hoping they connect with the right leader is a passive approach. Instead, get to know the leaders yourself. Sit in on a session or two. Ask your child specific questions: "What did your small group leader say about that topic? What did you think about their answer?" You're looking for leaders who encourage your child to think, not just comply.

Beyond church, think about the other environments your child already occupies. A coach who pulls your son aside after practice to talk about sportsmanship and effort is mentoring, whether they realize it or not. A music teacher who pushes your daughter past her comfort zone with patience and encouragement is building character in real time. Pay attention to which adults naturally draw your child's respect, and then invest in those relationships. Introduce yourself. Express gratitude. Invite them into your family's life in small ways, a dinner, a conversation, a thank-you note that makes clear you see what they're doing and value it.

You can also be direct with people you trust. Saying, "I'd love for my son to have more time around men who model what I'm trying to teach him. Would you be open to grabbing lunch with him once a month?" is straightforward and effective. Most quality people are honored by that kind of request. They just need to be asked.

One critical principle: mentors supplement your parenting. They don't replace it. If your child has a mentor they look up to, stay connected to that relationship. Check in with the mentor regularly. Ask your child what they're learning. The goal is a web of aligned influence, with you at the center, where every trusted adult is reinforcing the same core message from a slightly different angle. That consistency is powerful. Your child hears wisdom about integrity from you at the dinner table, then hears it again from a coach on the field, and again from a small group leader on Wednesday night. The repetition across multiple voices cements the principle in a way that your voice alone, no matter how strong, cannot.

Community Connections That Matter

Individual mentors are essential, but they work best inside a broader community of families who share your values. When your child grows up surrounded by other families operating from the same playbook, the standards you've set at home stop feeling like your family's isolated rules. They become the normal way people live.

Building this kind of community takes deliberate effort. It rarely assembles itself. Start with a simple scan of where your family already shows up. Your church congregation, your child's sports league, your neighborhood, the homeschool co-op, the volunteer organization. Within each of those circles, identify two or three families whose parenting approach aligns with yours. You don't need a perfect match. You need families who take faith seriously, who hold their kids to clear standards, and who parent with intention rather than by default.

Then do something most parents skip: pursue those families on purpose. Invite them over for a Friday night cookout. Organize a monthly family game night that rotates between homes. Set up a group text with three other parents from your child's school so you can coordinate on sleepovers, compare notes on social dynamics, and share information quickly. These connections don't need to be complicated. They need to be consistent. Showing up at the same table with the same people month after month builds the kind of relational depth that carries real weight when hard situations arise.

Strategic involvement in your child's activities adds another layer. When you volunteer as an assistant coach, a field trip chaperone, or a youth group helper, you gain two things: direct visibility into your child's social environment and relationship capital with the other adults in that space. You see who your child gravitates toward. You observe group dynamics firsthand. And you position yourself to influence the environment rather than just reacting to reports about it after the fact.

Building a support network for your own parenting is equally important. You need other parents you can call at ten o'clock on a Tuesday night when your daughter just told you something that knocked the wind out of you, and you're not sure how to respond. You need someone who'll tell you the truth when you're overreacting and back you up when you're right. Parenting in isolation makes every challenge feel bigger than it is and every decision feel uncertain. Parenting inside a trusted community of like-minded families gives you perspective, accountability, and reinforcement at the exact moments you need them most.

A practical approach: form or join a small parenting group of four to six couples from your church or neighborhood. Meet once a month. Pick a topic, share what's working, talk through what's hard, and pray for each other's families. This kind of structure keeps everyone sharpened and prevents the drift that happens when families try to go it alone.

Dealing with Negative Influences

Even with the best systems in place, harmful relationships will show up. Your child will connect with a peer who pulls them in the wrong direction, or an adult in a position of authority will model something that contradicts everything you've taught. Knowing how to respond with clarity and calm makes the difference between a temporary challenge and a lasting problem.

When you need to limit a harmful peer relationship, avoid making the other child the villain. That almost always backfires. Your child gets defensive, the forbidden friendship becomes more attractive, and you lose influence over the situation. Instead, use language that keeps the focus on your family's standards.

Try something like: "I've noticed that after you spend time with Marcus, you come home with an attitude that doesn't match who you are. We're going to take a break from hanging out for a while. That's my decision as your parent, and it's because I'm responsible for protecting the environment you grow in."

If your child pushes back, stay steady: "I understand you like Marcus, and I'm not saying he's a bad person. I'm saying the pattern I'm seeing after your time together tells me this friendship isn't helping you right now. That could change in the future, but right now, we're taking a step back."

For toxic peer groups, the most effective move is redirection rather than prohibition alone. Fill the gap. Enroll your child in a new activity. Arrange time with families from your inner circle. Create opportunities for new friendships to form in healthier environments. Kids resist a vacuum. They accept a replacement, especially when the replacement is genuinely enjoyable.

Playbook Implementation: Relationship Audit Checklist

Influence Evaluation Worksheet: List every person with regular access to your child. For each one, answer the three audit questions: What values do they model? How does my child behave after time with them? Do they support or undermine our family's standards? Assign each person a green, yellow, or red rating. Set a date to review in ninety days.

Community Connection Action Plan: Identify three families whose values align with yours. Reach out this week to schedule one shared meal or activity within the next thirty days. Choose one of your child's existing environments, whether it's a sports team, youth group, or school program, and commit to a volunteer role that gives you direct visibility. Set up a group text or monthly meetup with two to three trusted parents for ongoing support and accountability. Find one potential mentor for your child and make the ask within the next two weeks.

9

LAUNCHING STREET-SMART ADULTS: THE FINAL PLAYS FOR INDEPENDENCE

Your eleven-year-old asks to ride his bike to the park three blocks away to meet friends for a pickup basketball game. Your stomach tightens. A dozen questions fire through your mind: Who else will be there? What if something goes wrong? Is he ready for this? And underneath all of those practical concerns sits a deeper one you do not always say out loud: Am I ready to start letting go?

That tension is the defining challenge of this stretch. Everything you have built through discipline, decision-making training, peer pressure strategies, and honest conversations has been pointing toward one destination: a young person who can function without you standing over their shoulder.

The goal was never to keep your child close forever. It was to build someone strong enough to walk out the front door with their values intact, their thinking sharp, and their faith becoming their own. Which means the way you release control matters just as much as the way you held it.

The Gradual Release System

Freedom given too fast produces chaos. Freedom withheld too long breeds resentment or, worse, a young person who cannot handle basic decisions without calling you first. The sweet spot is a deliberate, structured release of responsibility and independence over time, tied directly to demonstrated maturity.

Think of it like a swimmer earning their way into the deep end. They do not jump into open water on day one. They prove competence at each stage: shallow end with a parent nearby, then treading water independently, then swimming laps without assistance. Each new privilege follows evidence that the previous skill has been mastered. Your approach to independence should follow the same logic.

Tie freedom to demonstrated responsibility. When your child consistently handles a smaller responsibility well, the next level of freedom opens up. That means you need clear, observable benchmarks rather than vague feelings about whether they are "mature enough." A twelve-year-old who manages their homework schedule for a full semester without reminders has shown you something concrete. That is different from a twelve-year-old who still needs daily check-ins. Same age, different readiness.

The practical framework looks like this: identify the specific freedom your child is requesting, or that you would like to extend. Then identify the responsibility that must come first. Make both explicit. Say it out loud.

"You want to ride your bike to the park without me. Here is what I need to see first: you follow the route we agreed on every time we ride together for two full weeks. You check in when you arrive. You come home at the time we set."

When they meet the benchmark, the freedom opens. When they do not, the timeline resets without drama or lectures. It is cause and effect, and they control the outcome.

Age-appropriate milestones give you a rough map for this progression. Between ages eight and nine, independence might look like walking to a neighbor's house alone for mature children in safe environments, managing a small amount of spending money, or choosing their own extracurricular activity from options you have pre-approved. Between ten and eleven, it expands to managing their own morning routine completely, handling small responsibilities like packing their own lunch, and resolving minor conflicts with friends without your intervention. Staying home alone for short errands may begin around eleven to twelve for some mature children, based on demonstrated readiness and local laws. By twelve, you are looking at things like biking to a friend's house independently, managing a small weekly budget, taking greater ownership of their homework schedule, and spending time in social environments like birthday parties or group outings where you are not in the room.

Each milestone carries a kingdom perspective when you frame it correctly. Managing spending money teaches stewardship. Resolving a disagreement with a friend without you stepping in builds the peacemaking muscle Jesus talked about in the Sermon on the Mount. Handling freedom responsibly reflects the principle in Luke 16:10 that faithfulness in small things leads to greater trust. You are not just teaching life skills. You are showing your child that God's design for growing up works the same way: prove faithful here, and more opens up.

The script for this is straightforward. "I'm increasing your freedom because you've earned it. You showed me you can handle X, so now you get Y. If Y goes well, Z comes next. And if it doesn't go well, we step back and try again. This isn't punishment. It's preparation."

One common mistake parents make is granting independence based on age alone. Your child turning ten does not automatically qualify them for staying home alone if they have not shown consistent responsibility with smaller freedoms first. Another mistake is pulling back freedom after a single slip. Kids will make errors during the release process. That is expected. The question is whether the error reflects a pattern or a one-time lapse. Patterns require a reset. Single lapses usually require a conversation and a second chance.

Preparing for Secular World Engagement

At some point, your child will spend growing portions of their day in environments you do not control. School classrooms. Sports teams. Friend groups at recess and in the neighborhood. The question is not whether they will encounter ideas and values that differ from yours. The question is whether they will know how to think clearly when they do.

Preparation for that engagement does not start in the teen years. It starts now, the moment you begin treating your home as a training ground for real-world pressure rather than a shelter from it.

This kind of readiness requires specific skills even at ages eight through twelve. Your child needs to know how to express what they believe and why, without getting defensive or shutting down. They need to understand that a teacher or classmate sharing a different perspective is not a personal attack. They need the ability to listen to someone else's viewpoint, notice where it differs from their own, and respond respectfully. These are skills you can practice at the dinner table long before the stakes get higher.

Try this exercise with your kids: pick a topic you know will come up at school or with friends, whether it is why your family believes in God, why certain rules matter, what makes something right or wrong, or why your family does things differently. Present a simple version of a different viewpoint. Then ask your child to respond. Coach them through it. Teach them to say things like, "I get why someone would think that. Here's what I believe, and here's why." This builds confidence without arrogance, which is exactly the posture that earns respect from peers and adults alike.

Maintaining faith outside your home depends on whether that faith is becoming your child's own or whether it still feels borrowed. This is the critical distinction even at this age. A child who goes to church only because you make them is building a habit, not a conviction. A child who is starting to wrestle with real questions, noticing God's faithfulness in their own experiences, and choosing small spiritual practices on their own is building something that will hold up when you are not standing next to them.

You can strengthen that ownership starting right now. First, stop answering every spiritual question for them. When they ask, "Why does God let bad things happen?" resist the urge to give the tidy answer. Instead, say, "That's one of the biggest questions out there. What do you think so far? What makes sense to you and what doesn't?" Let them build their own understanding with your guidance rather than your script.

Second, give them small choices within your faith community. If you have always picked their Sunday school class or kids' group, let them have a voice. "There are two groups meeting this semester. Which one interests you more?" This gets them used to evaluating spiritual environments and feeling ownership over their faith life, even while you are still guiding the bigger decisions.

Third, prepare them for being distinct without being isolated. The goal at school or in the neighborhood is not to win arguments or to blend in so completely that no one knows what they believe. The goal is to be present, kind, and clear.

Daniel in the Babylonian court is a powerful biblical model for this. He served with excellence. He earned trust and influence. He maintained his convictions without cutting himself off from everyone around him. And when the line was clear, he did not cross it. Teach your child that being around people who think differently is not a threat. Losing clarity about who they are while they are there is.

A helpful script for this: "You're going to be around kids who think very differently than you do. That's okay. You can learn from them, and they might learn something from you. Your job isn't to argue with everyone or to hide what you believe. Your job is to be kind, honest, and clear about where you stand. You'll know the moments when it matters."

The mistake to avoid here is fear-based preparation. If every conversation about school, friendships, or the outside world sounds like a warning about spiritual danger, your child will either become anxious or rebellious. Neither serves them well. Frame these environments as places where their faith can grow and be tested, not places to panic about. The difference in language changes everything about how they approach the experience.

Maintaining Connection Through Transitions

The shift from closely managing your child to gradually relating to them as a maturing young person is one of the hardest recalibrations you will face. The way you parent an eight-year-old needs to look noticeably different by the time they are twelve if you want to keep their trust and respect through the teen years ahead.

Staying engaged without hovering requires a gradual change in posture. You begin moving from director to coach. A director tells the actors where to stand, what to say, and when to move. A coach teaches the fundamentals, calls out what they see, and then lets the player make the play.

This shift feels uncomfortable because you still see the gaps. You still notice the choices that could go sideways. The discipline is choosing when to step in and when to let them work it out.

Here's a practical guide for that transition. Keep regular, low-pressure moments of connection. A nightly check-in at bedtime. A weekend walk or drive together. A shared activity you both enjoy, even if it is just ten minutes. The content of these interactions matters less than the consistency. You are communicating, "I'm here. I'm interested. I'm not going anywhere."

When your child shares a problem, start practicing the habit of listening before advising. With an older child in this range, try asking, "Do you want my help with this, or do you just need to talk it through?" That single question begins teaching them that you respect their growing ability to think for themselves.

Building toward a healthy, long-term relationship also means accepting that your child will increasingly make choices you would not make. Some of those choices will be genuinely wrong. Others will simply be different from your preferences. Learning to tell the difference now sets the stage for the teen years.

If your twelve-year-old picks a hobby that puzzles you, that is a preference difference. If they are consistently dishonest or gravitating toward harmful behavior, that is a values conversation. Reserve your strongest reactions for the moments that truly warrant them. If you treat every decision as a crisis, your voice becomes background noise precisely when they need to hear it most.

10

BRINGING IT ALL TOGETHER: YOUR ROADMAP FOR RAISING STREET-SMART KIDS

Ten chapters ago, you picked this up because something felt urgent. Maybe your child came home repeating an idea that didn't sit right. Maybe you watched them shrink under pressure from a friend group. Or maybe you simply looked at the world around you and thought, "I need a better plan." Whatever brought you here, you've now spent serious time building that plan. You've studied frameworks, practiced scripts, evaluated your own habits, and thought carefully about the kind of adult you're raising. That work matters. Before you move forward, it's worth pausing and pulling it all into one clear picture.

This chapter is your consolidated map. Think of it like a halftime review: the coach marks the key plays on the whiteboard, calls out what's working, and sends everyone back out with a focused game plan. You already know the material. Now you get to see how the pieces connect and tighten up the habits that will carry your family in the years ahead.

Summary of Core Principles and Frameworks

The foundation you've built rests on a tension most parenting advice mishandles. A lot of approaches lean hard in one direction: heavy on warmth and light on accountability, or heavy on rules and light on relationship. The system you've been working through holds both at full strength. High grace paired with high standards. That combination drives everything else.

You started by identifying your core values and separating them from flexible preferences. Core values are the non-negotiable biblical principles your family stands on. Preferences are the secondary choices that can shift with age, personality, and context. Keep that distinction sharp and your discipline stays targeted. Your child also stops experiencing every correction as an equal-weight crisis. Along the way, you built a family mission statement that puts those values into language your kids can remember and repeat. When decisions get messy, that language becomes the reference point.

Next came something a lot of parenting resources barely touch: your own emotional regulation. Before you can correct effectively, you have to manage your fear, frustration, and reactivity. The pause-and-pray discipline prep gives you a simple structure. You feel the surge, you pause, you pray briefly for wisdom, and then you respond instead of reacting. One small shift, big impact. It changes the atmosphere of a confrontation because your child sees what composure looks like under pressure when you model it.

The discipline framework itself centers on consequences that build character, not consequences that only punish behavior. That distinction matters more than most parents realize. Punitive discipline asks, "How do I make this stop?" Formative discipline asks, "What do I want my child to learn from this?" You practiced designing consequences that are connected to the behavior, proportional to the offense, and consistent over time. Those three qualities create a discipline culture your child can trust, even when they dislike the outcome.

Faith ownership was the next critical layer. You learned the difference between a child who performs belief on Sunday and a child who carries conviction into Monday. Sunday school knowledge gives kids the right answers to expected questions. Faith ownership gives them the ability to reason through unexpected ones. You built this by making room for honest questions, connecting Scripture to real situations your child actually faces, and letting them see your faith in action in ordinary, unscripted moments. The goal was never to produce a child who can recite verses on command. The goal was to develop a child whose faith functions as an internal compass when no one is watching.

Decision-making training extended that internal compass into practical territory. Instead of only telling your child what to do, you taught them how to think. The process involved helping them identify the real question behind a decision, weigh consequences before acting, consider who benefits and who gets hurt, and check the choice against their values. When your child practices this with small, everyday decisions, they build the mental muscle to use it when the stakes get higher.

The peer pressure playbook gave your child specific strategies for the social situations that trip up even confident kids. You practiced exit phrases, response scripts, and the idea of pre-deciding. Pre-deciding means your child has already made up their mind about certain scenarios before those scenarios happen. They know what they'll say if someone offers them something they don't want. They know how they'll respond if a friend pressures them to exclude someone. That kind of preparation takes the panic out of the moment and replaces it with a plan.

Internal validation ran through all of it. You worked to help your child locate their worth in their identity in Christ and in the values your family holds, rather than in peer approval or the metrics of social media. A child who knows who they are, and Whose they are, can absorb rejection without being wrecked by it. They can hear criticism without automatically believing it. They can stand in a room where everyone disagrees and still hold their ground, because their sense of self does not depend on the room's opinion.

Digital discipleship brought these principles into the day-to-day reality of screens and social media. You set boundaries around access and content, but you also taught your child how to think critically about what they consume online. You gave them tools for spotting manipulation, comparison traps, and algorithmic influence. The aim was not to raise a kid who avoids technology until they leave your house. It was to raise a kid who can use it wisely, with a working framework already in place.

Communication scripts for heavy topics gave you a practical toolkit for the conversations that feel the most intimidating. Sexuality, identity confusion, substance use, violence, injustice. You practiced starting these conversations proactively instead of waiting for a crisis to force your hand. The scripts gave you opening language, but the deeper principle was this: your child needs to know they can bring anything to you without the relationship breaking.

Building the inner circle focused on helping your child see the difference between acquaintances and true friends, connecting your family with mentors and community, and shaping an environment where your child's closest influences reinforce rather than erode your values. Launching toward independence gave you a roadmap for shifting from director to coach as your child matures, handing over responsibility in measured steps while keeping the relationship strong.

None of these frameworks stands alone. Emotional regulation supports effective discipline. Effective discipline builds the trust that makes faith conversations possible. Faith conversations form the internal compass that drives wise decision-making. Wise decision-making prepares your child for peer pressure. And a child who can handle peer pressure is a child who is becoming genuinely street-smart.

Final Encouragements for the Parenting Journey

You have a system now. You have language, frameworks, and strategies. And there will still be days when none of it seems to work.

Your thirteen-year-old will roll their eyes at the family mission statement. Your ten-year-old will forget every exit phrase you practiced and go along with the group anyway. You'll lose your composure during a discipline moment and say the exact thing you promised yourself you wouldn't say. That doesn't mean the system is failing. It means you're parenting real humans in real time.

Consistency matters more than perfection. The parent who shows up with the same values, the same warmth, and the same standards day after day creates something no single conversation can create: a pattern. Patterns are what children internalize. Your child may not remember the exact words you used on a random Tuesday night in October. They'll remember that you kept coming back to the same principles. They'll remember that correction was followed by connection. They'll remember a home that felt steady even when everything outside it didn't.

When you have a bad day, the next move is simple. Name it, correct course, and keep going. If you lost your temper, say so. "I handled that poorly. I'm sorry. Here's what I should have said." That kind of honesty does more for your child's growth than a flawless performance, because it teaches them that integrity includes owning your mistakes and making them right.

Proverbs 22:6 tells us to train up a child in the way they should go. The word "train" implies process. It implies repetition, adjustment, and time. You're planting seeds that will not all sprout on your schedule. Some of what you're teaching right now may take root during a college semester, during a hard season in their twenties, or the first time they face a real test with no one around to help. You might not see fruit right away. That's where trust in God's timing stops being a phrase and starts being a decision.

Grace applies to you, too. The same grace you're extending to your child when they mess up applies to your own parenting. God didn't call you to be a flawless parent. He called you to be a faithful one. Faithful means you keep showing up. It means you keep learning. It also means you ask for wisdom and trust that He provides it, even when you cannot see the full picture.

Celebrate the small wins along the way. Your child pushed back on a friend's idea instead of going along with it? That's growth. Your daughter asked you a hard question about something she saw online, instead of hiding it. That's the trust you've built. Your son admitted he made a bad choice before you found out about it? That's the internal compass starting to work. These moments usually aren't dramatic. They happen quietly, in passing, over dinner or in the car. Notice them. Say something. Let your child know you saw it.

Parenting also has a way of locking your eyes on the next problem, the next risk, the next thing that needs fixing. Some of what you're experiencing is natural; vigilance is part of the job. But if you never stop to recognize what's going right, you'll burn out. Worse, your child may start to feel like they never measure up, because all they hear is what still needs to change. Keep correcting, but make recognition a regular habit, too.

The cultural pressures your child faces are real, and they're intense. Social media algorithms are built to grab attention and shape thinking. Peer groups carry enormous influence during the tween and teen years. Messages from entertainment, advertising, and even some educational environments will often contradict what you're building at home. You're not imagining the challenge. It's significant.

Still, you are equipped to meet it. Every tool in this system was built for the world your child actually lives in. You're not relying on isolation to protect your child. You're building internal strength and wisdom so they can engage with the world and still hold their ground.

Keep your own faith active and visible. Your child is watching how you handle disappointment, conflict, uncertainty, and pressure. The way you respond to a difficult coworker, a financial setback, or a relational conflict teaches them more about applied faith than any lesson plan. You do not have to be dramatic about it. Let them see you pray before a hard conversation. Let them hear you say how a passage of Scripture shaped your thinking about a real situation. Let them watch you choose integrity when a shortcut is available. That lived example is one of the strongest teaching tools you have.

Action Steps to Start Today

Knowledge without execution stays theoretical. The difference between parents who see real change and parents who feel frustrated six months from now usually comes down to consistent follow-through. Here is how to move from understanding to action.

Start by reviewing the playbook exercises from each chapter, one chapter per week. Set a recurring time on your calendar for this. Sunday evenings work well for many families, but pick whatever slot you will actually protect (I tend to do better with a set time than a vague "sometime this weekend"). During that weekly review, read through the key framework from one chapter, identify one specific exercise or practice, and apply it during the coming week. You don't need to implement everything at once. Stack one practice on top of another over a ten-week cycle, and give each tool time to settle in before you add the next one.

Pull out the scripts and practice them out loud. This sounds awkward, and it is at first. Do it anyway. Practicing a response to peer pressure with your child at the kitchen table makes it far more likely they'll use that response at school. Run through scenarios together. "What would you say if someone asked you to share answers on a test?" "What would you do if your friend group started making fun of someone?" Keep it conversational. You can even keep it a little playful. The goal is familiarity, so the words show up under pressure instead of disappearing in the moment.

Use the scripts proactively, not reactively. One of the biggest mistakes parents make with communication tools is waiting for a crisis to dig them out. By then, emotions are high, and the conversation is already uphill. Bring up difficult topics during calm, ordinary moments instead. Mention something you read about social media influence while you're making dinner together. Ask your child what they'd do in a hypothetical scenario during a car ride. Low-pressure conversations build the relational muscle that makes high-pressure conversations possible.

Engage your community and support systems deliberately. Identify two or three families whose values align with yours and build a regular connection with them. This could be a monthly dinner, a shared small group, or simply coordinated activities so your kids spend time with peers who reinforce good habits. Talk to your church leadership about whether mentoring structures exist for your child's age group. If they don't, consider helping start one. A child who has three or four trusted adults in their life besides their parents has a dramatically stronger safety net than a child who has only two.

Find or form an accountability circle for yourself as a parent. This can be as simple as one other parent you text weekly with an honest update. "Here's what went well this week. Here's where I struggled. Here's what I'm working on next." Parenting in isolation leads to drift. Having even one person who knows your goals and checks in with you creates a level of intentionality that's hard to maintain alone.

Put the decision-making framework on your refrigerator or somewhere your child sees it daily. Write it out in simple language that they can reference. When a decision comes up, point to it. Over time, they'll internalize the process without needing the paper. The same principle applies to your family mission statement. Post it where it's visible. Reference it in real conversations. "Does this choice line up with what we said matters to our family?" Asked consistently, that question trains your child's mind to filter decisions through values rather than impulse.

Set a ninety-day checkpoint. Mark it on your calendar right now. Ninety days from today, sit down and evaluate. Which practices have become habits? Which ones dropped off? Where have you seen growth in your child? Where do you still see gaps? Adjust your approach based on what you observe. Parenting is iterative. What works perfectly for your ten-year-old today may need modification when they're twelve. The frameworks stay the same, but the application shifts as your child grows.

Finally, pray with specificity. Pray over each area covered in this system. Pray for your child's friendships by name. Pray for wisdom in the conversations you know are coming. Pray for the situations you can't predict. Pray for your own patience, consistency, and discernment. James 1:5 promises that God gives wisdom generously to those who ask. Ask. Regularly. Specifically. Out loud when your child can hear it, and silently when they can't.

You picked this up because you wanted more than hope. You wanted a plan, and now you have one. Start small, stay consistent, and keep your expectations realistic. Then reassess, because what your child needs this season may look different in the next one.

11

FAQS AND TROUBLESHOOTING: OVERCOMING COMMON CHALLENGES

Your twelve-year-old just slammed her bedroom door hard enough that the family photos rattled on the hallway wall. Ten minutes ago, you calmly explained why she couldn't attend a sleepover at a friend's house where you knew there'd be zero adult supervision. You used the communication framework. You stayed measured. You offered an alternative. She still looked at you like you'd ruined her entire life. Now you're standing in the kitchen, coffee going cold, wondering if any of this actually works.

It does. Still, even the best system runs into friction. Kids test boundaries because that's part of growing up. Culture pushes back because that's what culture does. And you hit walls because you're a human being carrying a heavy responsibility. The strategies throughout this material are meant for real life, which means they have to handle the messy parts, too. This chapter walks through the most common stumbling blocks parents face when putting these principles into practice and gives you clear, specific ways to move through each one.

Handling Resistance and Setbacks

Pushback from your child is normal. Read that again. A kid who never resists, never questions, and never pushes a boundary is often either deeply compliant out of fear or simply hasn't been tested yet. When your son crosses his arms and says, "That's so unfair," or your daughter rolls her eyes and mutters under her breath, that's often a sign the system is doing something. You've drawn a line, and they're bumping into it. The goal was never to raise a child who unquestioningly agrees with everything you say. The goal is to raise one who learns how to handle disagreement, respect authority, and eventually think through hard situations with wisdom.

Even so, resistance is exhausting when you're in the middle of it.

The Core Problem

Pushback often includes emotional protest, such as tears, anger, or dramatic reactions, logical challenges like "But everyone else gets to" or "You don't trust me," and passive resistance, which might involve ignoring the rule, doing the minimum, or slow compliance with a bad attitude. Each one calls for a slightly different response, but all three share the same root issue: your child is testing whether the boundary holds. If it does, they learn security. If it doesn't, they learn that enough pressure makes the rules bend.

What to Do When They Push Back Emotionally

When your child erupts, your first job is managing your own response. Proverbs 15:1 puts it plainly: "A gentle answer turns away wrath." That doesn't mean you get soft or permissive. It means you stay steady. If your child is yelling, lower your voice. If they're crying in frustration, name the emotion without reversing the decision. Try: "I can see you're really upset about this. I get it. The answer is still no, and here's why it matters." You're validating the feeling while holding the line. Kids need to learn that big emotions don't change the outcome and that disappointment, while miserable, is survivable.

A common mistake is getting pulled into a back-and-forth debate at the emotional peak. Your child isn't processing logic when they're flooded with frustration. Save the deeper conversation for later. Say, "We can talk about this more when we're both calm. Right now, the decision stands." Then do what you said you would do. Come back within an hour or two and have the real conversation when both of you can think clearly.

What to Do When They Challenge Your Logic

"Why can't I? Jake's parents let him." This one hits a nerve because it makes you feel like the outlier, the strict parent, the one who's out of touch. Here, your family values framework does the heavy lifting. You don't need to defend your decision against every other household's standards. You've already decided what your family stands for. So your response can sound like this: "I hear you. Other families make different choices, and that's their call. In our family, we've agreed on what matters to us, and this fits that." You're not taking a shot at the other family. You're simply staying in your lane.

If your child brings a genuinely good argument to the table, listen. There's a difference between whining for a different outcome and making a thoughtful case. If your thirteen-year-old says, "Mom, I know you're worried about supervision, but what if I FaceTime you at 9 PM and you talk to Jake's mom beforehand?" that's problem-solving, and it deserves consideration. Taking good reasoning seriously doesn't weaken your authority. It strengthens it because your child learns that respectful communication actually has weight in your house.

Adjusting Discipline Without Losing Authority

Sometimes a consequence you set doesn't fit the situation as well as you thought it would. Maybe you grounded your son for two weeks over something that probably warranted three days. Here's the truth: changing a consequence can be fine if you do it with transparency. What erodes trust is changing it under pressure. So if you need to adjust, do it on your terms, not in the middle of a meltdown. Wait until things are calm, then say, "I've thought about this more, and I think two weeks was too much for what happened. I'm adjusting it to one week. The behavior still wasn't okay, and this consequence still stands."

That kind of honesty builds credibility. It teaches your child that leaders can recalibrate without being weak.

Common Mistakes to Avoid

Giving in during the heat of the moment just to end the conflict. This trains your child that persistence beats principle. Raising your voice to match theirs turns a discipline moment into a power struggle nobody wins. And the silent-treatment approach, where you withdraw emotionally to punish them, damages the connection without teaching anything useful. Stay present. Stay calm. Stay consistent.

Quick Action Step: The next time your child pushes back on a boundary, pause for five seconds before responding. Use that pause to choose one calm, clear sentence. Practice this once this week, even on a small issue, so it shows up when the bigger moments hit.

Balancing Faith and Cultural Pressures

Your child can spend 30 to 40 hours or more per week under the influence of people who don't share your values, including school, sports, extracurriculars, and neighborhood friendships. That's a significant chunk of their waking life absorbing different perspectives, different standards, and different definitions of what's normal. This isn't automatically bad. Exposure to the broader world is part of growing up. But it does create tension, especially when your child comes home repeating ideas that cut against what you've been teaching.

The Core Problem

The real challenge isn't that your child hears different viewpoints. It's that they don't always have the tools to weigh those viewpoints well. A ten-year-old who hears a classmate say, "The Bible is just a bunch of old stories," doesn't have a theological response ready. They just feel awkward and unsure. A twelve-year-old whose friend group treats certain behaviors as no big deal starts wondering if maybe their family is the one that's wrong. The pressure usually isn't dramatic. It's subtle, steady, and social.

Responding to Conflicting Values at School

When your child comes home with a question or comment that shows a clash between what they're hearing and what they've been taught, resist the urge to react with alarm. If you treat every conflicting idea as a crisis, your child will stop bringing those conversations to you. Treat it as a moment for coached thinking instead.

Your son says, "My teacher said there's no real proof God exists." Instead of launching into an apologetics lecture, try this: "That's interesting. What did you think when she said that?" Let him talk. Then guide the conversation: "What would you say is your strongest reason for believing God is real?" You're helping him examine the claim and put words to his own conviction. That's how faith shifts from inherited belief to personal ownership.

With younger kids, keep it simple: "Some people believe different things than we do, and you'll see that your whole life. What we believe is based on God's Word. Let's talk about why."

Navigating Sensitive Topics Respectfully

Some cultural conversations are more loaded than others. Your child will run into topics related to identity, sexuality, family structure, and morality that the broader culture treats very differently than Scripture does. The temptation is to either avoid these topics altogether or come in so hot that your child feels anxious instead of equipped.

A better approach is preemptive and measured. If you know a topic is likely to come up at school or online, address it at home first. Use age-appropriate language and a tone that communicates confidence without hostility. "You might hear kids at school talking about [topic]. Here's what our family believes, and here's why. You might meet people who see it differently, and we treat everyone with kindness and respect, even when we disagree." That framing gives your child both conviction and compassion, which they'll need if they're going to hold their ground without getting harsh or defensive.

A practical script for when your child asks about a sensitive cultural issue: "I'm glad you brought this to me. Here's what the Bible teaches about it. Some people see this differently, and we can respect them as people while still holding to what we believe is true. Does that make sense? What questions do you have?"

Strengthening Your Child's Biblical Worldview

A worldview isn't built in a single conversation. It's built over hundreds of small moments. One of the most effective ways to strengthen it is to bring biblical thinking into everyday situations. When you watch a movie together, ask, "What values was that character living by? How does that compare to what Scripture says?" When a news story comes up, ask, "How would you think about that through what we believe?" Those quick conversations often do more than a formal lesson because they train your child to run life through a biblical filter without needing a prompt.

Family devotions help, but they work best when they're interactive instead of lecture-based. Let your child ask hard questions. Let them express doubt. A child who can voice doubt in a safe environment is less likely to go hunting for answers in an unsafe one. James 1:5 reminds us that God gives wisdom generously to those who ask. Teach your children to ask, not to perform.

Common Mistakes to Avoid

Demonizing everyone who disagrees with your values. This creates an "us vs. them" mentality that isolates your child socially and makes faith feel like a bunker instead of something solid to stand on. Assuming your child's school is the enemy is another one. Many teachers are well-meaning people doing their best, even if their perspective differs from yours. Also, watch the impulse to overreact when your child expresses doubt or curiosity about a different viewpoint. Curiosity is often the beginning of conviction, not the end of it.

Quick Action Step: This week, ask your child one open-ended question about something they've heard at school or from friends that surprised them. Listen all the way through before you respond. Use it as a coaching moment, not a correction moment.

Keeping Momentum Going

Six weeks into implementing a new parenting approach, the initial energy fades. The family meetings feel repetitive. The scripts start sounding mechanical. Your child's progress seems to plateau, and you catch yourself sliding back into old patterns. You start wondering if the effort is worth it.

This is a dangerous phase because the temptation to quit shows up disguised as realism. "Maybe this just doesn't work for our family." "Maybe my kid is different." "Maybe I'm overthinking this." Those thoughts feel reasonable, but they're often fatigue talking. Fatigue has answers.

Avoiding Burnout as a Parent

Parenting burnout often arises when emotional and physical output consistently exceeds replenishment, leading to exhaustion. You're giving correction, guidance, emotional energy, and spiritual leadership day after day, and it can feel like nothing is coming back. It helps to name what you're actually doing here: you're playing the long game. The results of what you're doing now often won't show up for months or even years. That doesn't mean nothing is happening. A tree doesn't show its roots, but that's what keeps it upright when the weather turns.

Burnout prevention starts with being honest about your limits. You don't have to have a deep, meaningful conversation with your child every single day. Some days you're just getting through homework and bedtime, and that's fine. The framework is something you return to. It's not a demand for perfection.

Build recovery time into your week. It looks different for every parent. For some, it's thirty minutes alone with a cup of coffee before the house wakes up (I still think this is one of the cheapest forms of sanity). For others, it's a weekly phone call with a friend who understands the weight you're carrying. For many, it's time in prayer and Scripture that steadies your own spirit before you try to pour into someone else's. Jesus himself withdrew from the crowds to pray. If he kept that rhythm of engagement and rest, you can too.

Share the load, too. If you have a spouse, make sure you're both carrying the weight of intentional parenting. Check in regularly about what's working, what's not, and who needs a break. If you're parenting solo, lean on your community, whether that's a church small group, a trusted family member, or a mentor who can offer perspective when you're running low.

Setting Realistic Expectations

One of the fastest routes to discouragement is measuring your child's growth against an unrealistic standard. If you expect your eleven-year-old to respond perfectly to every boundary, every conversation, and every moral challenge, you'll always feel like you're failing. Kids are works in progress. So are you.

Realistic expectations sound like this: "My child will still make mistakes, but they'll make fewer of the same mistakes over time." "My child won't always agree with me, but they'll know they can come to me." "Some weeks will feel like we're moving backward, and that's part of the process." These aren't lowered standards. They're honest benchmarks that keep you grounded.

A helpful practice is to keep a simple log. Once a week, jot down one thing your child did that showed growth, even if it's small. Maybe your daughter paused before reacting to her brother's teasing. Maybe your son brought up a question about something he saw online instead of hiding it. These moments are easy to miss when you're staring at the big picture, but they're the kind of evidence you want to notice.

Celebrating Incremental Growth

Growth in character and faith rarely shows up as a dramatic transformation. It shows up in small shifts. Your child chooses honesty when lying would have been easier. They walk away from a conversation that was going somewhere unhealthy. They ask to pray about a decision instead of reacting on impulse. Those wins matter, and they're worth naming.

When you see growth, say it out loud. "I noticed you handled that situation with your friend really well today. That took maturity, and I respect it." Specific praise tied to character builds internal motivation. Over time, your child starts to see themselves as someone who can make wise choices, and that identity tends to reinforce itself.

You can mark progress as a family, too. It doesn't have to be elaborate. A special dinner, a later bedtime on Friday, a simple acknowledgment at the table: "I want to recognize something I saw this week." Small rituals like that help balance out how much space correction and discipline naturally take up.

Galatians 6:9 says, "Let us not become weary in doing good, for at the proper time we will reap a harvest if we do not give up." That verse isn't just about spiritual work in the abstract. It's about Tuesday night at the dinner table when you're tired, your kid is distracted, and you still choose to show up.

Common Mistakes to Avoid

- Comparing your family's progress to other families, especially the curated versions you see at church or on social media.
- Abandoning the whole system because one part felt clunky; adjust the part that isn't working and keep the rest.
- And the biggest one: waiting until you feel motivated to keep going. Motivation tends to follow action, not the other way around. Do the next right thing even when it feels flat, then reassess once you're rested.

Quick Action Step: Tonight or this weekend, tell your child one specific thing you've noticed them do well recently. Make it about character, not performance. Then write down one area where you've seen your own growth as a parent over the past month.

CONCLUSION

You picked up this playbook because something in your gut told you the stakes are too high to wing it. That instinct was right. The world your child is growing up in moves faster, speaks louder, and pushes harder than anything you faced at their age. And yet, here you are, still in the fight. That matters more than you probably give yourself credit for.

Let's be honest about what you've built over the course of these chapters. You haven't just collected tips or memorized scripts. You've put together a working system. A framework for discipline that actually builds character instead of just managing behavior. A communication approach that keeps the door open even when conversations get uncomfortable. A strategy for helping your child think through decisions on their own rather than just following your rules until they leave the house. None of that is small. None of that is accidental.

The foundation you laid early on, clarifying your core values and learning to regulate your own emotions before correcting your child, that's what holds everything else together. Without it, every strategy in this playbook would feel like a loose tool rattling around in a toolbox. With it, you have a coherent way to parent that doesn't shift based on your mood, your child's latest outburst, or whatever cultural trend showed up on their feed this morning.

From there, you built outward. You learned how to make faith something your child owns rather than something they perform on Sunday and forget by Monday afternoon. You practiced responding to peer pressure scenarios before they happened, giving your child language and confidence they can actually use in the hallway or the group chat. You developed a plan for screens and social media that goes beyond "just say no" and actually teaches discernment. And you equipped yourself with scripts for the heavy conversations you used to dread, the ones about identity, honesty, relationships, and the kind of choices that shape who your child becomes.

Those aren't abstract ideas. They're tools you can put to work tonight. Tomorrow morning. This weekend, when your kid pushes back on a boundary, you feel that familiar tension rise in your chest.

Here's something worth remembering as you move forward. Your child doesn't need you to be perfect. They need you to be present, consistent, and willing to repair when things go sideways. Some of your best parenting moments will come right after your worst ones, when you circle back, own your reaction, and model exactly the kind of humility and honesty you're trying to build in them. That's not failure. That's the system working.

Proverbs 22:6 says, "Train up a child in the way he should go, and when he is old he will not depart from it." That verse carries a promise, but it also carries a weight. Training isn't passive. It's repetitive, intentional, and sometimes exhausting. You won't always see the fruit of it in real time. Your twelve-year-old probably won't thank you for the boundaries you held this week. Your nine-year-old may not fully understand why you're teaching her to evaluate what her friends say instead of just going along. But the seeds are going into the ground. Every conversation, every corrected course, every moment you chose connection over convenience planted something.

The culture your child walks through every day is not going to slow down for your family. Social media algorithms won't pause because your kid needs more time to develop discernment. Peer groups won't wait until your child is "ready" to test their values. That's precisely why you can't afford to wait either. The playbook is in your hands. The strategies are specific. The next step is always the same: pick one thing and do it today.

Maybe that means sitting down tonight and having the five-minute check-in you've been putting off. Maybe it means revisiting your family's screen agreement with fresh clarity. Maybe it means simply telling your child, "I noticed something good in you this week," and naming it with specifics. Start where you are. Use what you've learned. Trust the process even when the progress feels invisible.

You are not raising a child who merely survives the pressures of this world. You are raising someone who can see clearly, think independently, and stand firm when everyone around them is drifting. Someone whose faith isn't borrowed from you but rooted in their own understanding of who God is and what He asks of them. Someone who can walk into any room, any school, any situation, and know who they are without needing approval from the crowd.

That's the kind of kid who changes the culture instead of being shaped by it. And that work started the moment you decided to be intentional about how you parent.

Keep showing up. Keep having the hard conversations. Keep adjusting, praying, and doing the next right thing. You're more equipped than you were when you started, and your child is more prepared than they know. The plays are drawn up. Now go run them.

www.ingramcontent.com/pod-product-compliance
Lightning Source LLC
Chambersburg PA
CBHW061004050726

47592CB00003B/1331